All the Wisdom and None of the Junk:
Secrets of Applying for College Admission and Scholarships is a publication of the
Boettcher Foundation.

Based in Denver, Colorado, the Boettcher Foundation is a private philanthropic
foundation that invests in the promise of Colorado and the potential of
Coloradans. The Boettcher Foundation Scholarship is a full-ride scholarship
awarded to graduating high-school seniors who are selected based on academics,
service, leadership and character. Recipients can use their scholarship at the
Colorado college or university of their choice.

At Boettcher we believe in investing in the most talented citizens because
supporting their hard work and leadership will enable them to give back to their
communities for years to come. This book is an effort to demystify the scholarship
selection process and further support our mission by helping the next generation
of talented citizens apply for college and scholarships.

This book is not specific only to the Boettcher Foundation Scholarship, and is
based on both our insights and those gained from many of our colleagues in the
scholarship and college admissions community.

ALL THE WISDOM AND NONE OF THE JUNK: SECRETS OF APPLYING FOR COLLEGE ADMISSION AND SCHOLARSHIPS

By Katy Craig and Katie Kramer

Reach new heights

boettcher
FOUNDATION®

BoettcherFoundation.org

Praise for
All the Wisdom and None of the Junk:
Secrets of Applying for College Admission and Scholarships

"It's remarkable how much useful information is packed into such a condensed manual--all delivered in mercifully accessible prose. Also, the authors' meticulousness is notable--the organization of the book makes following its prescriptions easy and should go a long way toward unburdening the applicant of both tedium and nervousness. ... A clear and practical resource, intelligently structured."

- Kirkus Reviews

"This is THE book for college-bound students. It should also sit firmly on the shelves of all high school guidance counselors and others involved in helping students navigate the often-challenging application process."

- Blue Ink Review

"The book's tone is frank but encouraging, and students and parents who use it will be better informed about how to put forth a stellar application packet."

- Foreword Reviews

"Finally, the book that provides detailed insights into the college and scholarship application process. Go behind the scenes and understand what committees are really looking for in your application. The authors, experts in college scholarships, give powerful advice on how best to present yourself to colleges and scholarship programs.

Get this book and lower your anxiety about the application process!"

– J. Mark Davis, President, Coca-Cola Scholars Foundation

"All the Wisdom and None of the Junk helps demystify the admission and scholarship application processes that millions of students and families struggle with each year. It's a pragmatic path that any student can benefit from knowing."

– Kevin Byrne, Managing Director, U.S. Programs, Michael & Susan Dell Foundation

"I highly recommend this book for students and families; there are many takeaways and tips to set you apart. As a higher education administrator and former admissions officer, I know that colleges are looking for academically-talented students who will be great citizens in the community. All the Wisdom and None of the Junk will help you show them why you are a great candidate!"

– Jennifer McDuffie, Assistant Dean of Students, University of Colorado Boulder

"Increased competition to earn scholarships and admission to top colleges has turned most students' senior year of high school into an anxiety-ridden roller-coaster. This book relieves the fear with clear guidance on how to prepare, who to ask for help, where to find resources and most importantly, how to tell your story effectively. … Read this book and take the guesswork out of college admissions and scholarships."

– Anne Lassen, Assistant Vice President, Flinn Scholars Program

"I love this book. It's a useful and practical guide for any student who is applying for competitive colleges or scholarships. The examples and analysis make clear what students should do, and, just as importantly, what students should not do. I will have a copy of this book on my shelf to use as a reference with my students!"

– Adam Silver, Vice President, Denver Test Prep

"This book provides students detailed strategies for college and scholarship essays. The authors give students clear examples of strong writing, as well as examples of what not to provide. For students completing the Common Application, this book guides you in completing all written sections, and helps you to better understand what colleges and scholarship organizations need to hear. … I highly recommend this tool!"

– Rena Maez, Lead College Advisor, Thomas Jefferson High School, Denver Scholarship Foundation

"I have spent the last 15 years working in the field of scholarships and have studied many scholarship programs and read many scholarship applications. … The authors are correct, this arduous process requires knowing the basics AND a willingness to self-reflect, ask for help and to look outside of yourself for perspective, all challenging for people of any age. This book will be front and center in my office and will soon have dog-eared pages. Thank you for this valuable resource!"

– Amy Weinstein, Executive Director, National Scholarship Providers Association (NSPA)

All the Wisdom and None of the Junk:
Secrets of Applying for College Admission and Scholarships

TABLE OF CONTENTS

I. AUTHORS' NOTE

We believe college and scholarship applications are needlessly shrouded in mystery, and that students have a right to understand a process that radically affects their lives. Our intent is that the information and specific strategies in this book will be directly useful to you.

– Katy Craig and Katie Kramer

II. HOW TO USE THIS BOOK

This book takes you step by step through the college and scholarship application process, using actual prompts and sample responses to the Common Application (accepted by nearly 700 colleges and universities) and the Boettcher Scholarship Application (for more information on the Boettcher Scholarship and the Boettcher Foundation – where we've worked for years, giving students full-ride scholarships – see the foundation website at www.boettcherfoundation.org). While the text and examples come from one or the other application, the strategies we impart are valuable whether you're completing the Common App (as it is commonly referred to), an institution-specific college or university application or a scholarship application.

The chapters are organized in accordance with the order of most applications – starting with overall information, then moving into the activity section, followed by the short-answer questions and application essay. This way you can have just-in-time advice as you work your way from the start of your application to the finish.

III. BASICS PEOPLE ASSUME YOU KNOW BUT YOU JUST MIGHT NOT

1. GET YOUR GAME FACE ON:
THE APPLICATION PROCESS WILL FEEL REALLY LONG

The application process is going to feel really long. It is. Knowing that up front will help you pace yourself and nail each individual application.

Most students complete their college applications in the fall of their senior year. If you've had the chance to start your personal essays in the spring of your junior year, congrats—you're ahead of the curve and will benefit greatly from the extra time you have for editing. That said, if you haven't started the essays, don't fret. Our chapter on essays will get you there as you dig in during fall semester.

But be forewarned: as welcome as winter break senior year always is, it's just a break. There is more to be done when you return to school.

At the beginning of spring semester you'll want to complete your final college applications for regular admission and, most importantly, hit the scholarship applications hard for those with spring deadlines. Even if you've applied for a number of scholarships, you'll want to do as many as you reasonably can. If you end up finding yourself in the extraordinary position of having more financial aid than what it costs you to attend college, you can always decline the scholarships that you win but don't need. It can be more difficult, though, to find scholarships once you've enrolled in college. **Your best chance of earning money for college is to stay focused and secure it during your senior year of high school.**

The table below outlines what to be thinking about and doing each year of high school. If you've missed a step, don't worry. Just pick up where you are and move forward from there, knowing that counselors and college access advisors are a great help in making up for lost time.

When	What to Do

Fall Semester Freshman and Sophomore Years	• Meet with your high school counselor and/or college access advisor to
	  ◊ discuss your interests and college plans
	  ◊ ensure you're taking a course load that's preparing you for college

When	What to Do

Fall Semester Junior Year, if possible	• Meet with your high school counselor and/or college access advisor to
	  ◊ discuss your interests and college plans
	  ◊ ensure you're taking a course load that's preparing you for college
	  ◊ begin drafting a college and scholarship list
	  ◊ see if any of the schools you're considering have weekend or summer programs for you to try (which may be free for first-generation or low income students).
	• Parents/guardians, teachers, coaches, religious/spiritual leaders or other people you turn to for advice and support are also great to talk to about your college application process – see section four of this chapter for more on finding people to help you
	  ◊ While you're thinking about who in your life can support you in your college and scholarship search, begin thinking about who you might ask for a letter of recommendation. Look at the requirements of the schools and scholarships you're considering to see how many letters they require and ask yourself who might best represent you. Typically, applications won't ask for more than three letters of rec, in which case we recommend asking for one from your high school counselor or college access advisor, one from a teacher and one from an extra-curricular advisor, community member or boss. That way, each recommender will speak to a different part of you and round out your application.
	• In deciding where to apply to college, research a number of schools and look at
	  ◊ The type of school (two-year, four-year, private/public)
	  ◊ Its location, size, student body and professors
	  ◊ Which majors are available – if you've chosen one, make sure it's available, and if you're undecided, make sure they have a few majors in your top few interests
	  ◊ How hard it is to get accepted and how your grades and test scores compare to institutional averages
	  ◊ Graduation rates – one of the key factors in earning a bachelor's degree is whether the school graduates its students. Keep your eye on the prize of not just enrolling, but graduating from your chosen institution in a reasonable (and affordable) amount of time.
	  ◊ Academic support/disability services that may be helpful to you
	  ◊ Sports and activities that you'd like to pursue
	  ◊ Cost of attendance - remember that
	    - you can apply for financial aid and scholarships to lower the actual cost to you
	    - cost of attendance is more than just tuition – it also includes books, fees, room and board…and needs to be multiplied by the number of years that you anticipate needing to earn your degree

When	What to Do
Fall Semester Junior Year, if possible (*continued*)	◊ NOTE: it pays to be wary of trade/vocational schools that offer certificates or Associate's Degrees. Many are proprietary schools, which means they are for-profit institutions trying to make money by admitting students (and, presumably, keeping them in school). This is not always the case, but it does happen fairly often, so it's worth doing your research and checking with your counselor or college access advisor about any for-profit institutions you're considering (this is also why it's important to check graduation rates). It may be that in your particular situation, community colleges are a better option because they offer Associate's Degrees at significantly lower rates than those for-profit institutions seeking to make a considerable income. • Continue your extra-curricular activities, consider adding one or two more that are meaningful to you and taking on some leadership positions in those that you most enjoy (for more on the impact of breadth and depth of extracurricular involvement on college and scholarship acceptance, see Chapters V and VI).

Spring Semester Junior Year	• Take the SAT and/or ACT.
	  ◊ Remember that SAT fee waivers are available to low-income 11th and 12th grade students in the U.S. or U.S. territories. These waivers cover
	    - the registration fee for up to two SATs, with or without the SAT Essay
	    - the fee for up to two SAT Subject tests
	    - four limited-time score reports, plus four score reports to be used at any time
	    - a CSS (College Scholarship Service) Profile waiver. NOTE: these waivers are difficult to obtain without the SAT fee waiver, and the CSS Profile is required by many private colleges and universities to determine your eligibility for non-government financial aid.
	  ◊ Also note that ACT fee waivers are available to U.S. citizens who are enrolled in 11th or 12th grade, testing in the U.S., U.S. Territories or Puerto Rico and meet one or more of ACT's requirements of economic need (which you can view online at the ACT website). These waivers cover:
	    - the registration fee for either the ACT (no writing) or the ACT with writing
	    - one report to the high school and up to four college choices
	• Start the application essay.
	• Contact program officers and admission representatives of colleges an scholarships in which you're particularly interested.
	  ◊ This may feel uncomfortable, but trust us, just starting your interaction by telling them that you're interested in their scholarship or institution will lead these representatives to be happy to hear from you.

When	What to Do
Spring Semester Junior Year (*continued*)	◊ Share the information you've found online or through conversations you've had with those helping you in order to share your plan for applying (this gives them the opportunity to fill in any information you may be missing) ◊ End by asking any questions that you may have or saying that you look forward to applying. • Visit colleges if at all possible (ask admission representatives at your top-choice schools about travel assistance or visit programs for low-income students, if applicable). • Talk with your high school counselor and/or college access advisor to make sure your senior year schedule is preparing you for college (and college applications) • Register to retake the SAT and/or ACT in summer or fall NOTE: you need to register six or more weeks before the exam date (see above note on waivers for low-income students), and ACT has done studies that show 57% of students increase their score between their first and second times taking the exam.

Fall Semester Senior Year	• Retake the SAT and/or ACT if you didn't already retake it in the summer (see above note on waivers for low-income students).
	• Seek increasing levels of leadership in your school and community activities.
	• Start/finish the application essay and have friends and mentors read it (see section four of this chapter for information on how to identify "your people" to help you through the process.
	• Submit the FAFSA (Free Application for Federal Student Aid).
	• Meet with your high school counselor and/or college access advisor to make sure you're on track to meet graduation requirements, discuss your college and scholarship list and ask for a letter of recommendation.
	• Ask for other letters of recommendation from teachers or employers and make sure to
	   ◊ give them at least two weeks' notice
	   ◊ provide them with the selection criteria of the colleges/scholarships to which you're applying
	   ◊ remind them of deadlines – it is absolutely OK to check in with recommenders to see if they need any additional information from you and are remembering the deadlines. Just like you, they're busy. Despite their best intentions, recommenders may forget to write letters.
	   ◊ follow-up with a thank you note once the deadline comes around
	   ◊ let them know of any admission or selection decisions
	• Ask for electronic test scores to be sent to any colleges or scholarship providers that request them. Do this well in advance of application deadlines, because it can take weeks for scores to be received by schools. Do not assume that because scores are on your transcript that they will be accepted.

When	What to Do

Fall Semester Senior Year (*continued*)	• Work on applications for both colleges (early admission or decision) and scholarships with fall deadlines, and start the financial aid application process.
	  ◊ If you're trying to decide how many schools to apply to, between three and seven is a good rule of thumb, with all of them meeting the criteria of which type, size, etc. you've chosen. In addition, you should choose at least one and preferably two in each of the following categories:
	    - Schools for which you are highly competitive because your grades and test scores are above their published averages
	    - Schools for which you are competitive because your grades and test scores are about the same as their published averages
	    - Schools for which you are less competitive because your grades and test scores are below their published averages
	  ◊ Also make sure that at least one of these schools is one for which you know you will be able to get enough financial aid to attend (while also keeping in mind that those institutions with higher listed costs may offer you enough financial aid to become your most affordable options)
	• Research scholarships with spring deadlines.
	• If you receive initial declines or wait list status, request feedback on what you could do to strengthen future applications or interviews, being friendly and courteous at each stage. You never know if a finalist in a selection process is going to withdraw, leaving you next in line. Make sure every interaction you have with organizations leaves them thinking well of you.

Spring Semester Senior Year	• Finish and submit college applications for regular admission and applications for scholarships with spring deadlines.
	• Ask your high school counseling office to send your first semester transcripts to any institutions that have requested them.
	• Keep focusing on your classes. College and scholarship offers are often contingent on finishing the year with a strong academic record.
	• Compare financial aid packages (checking to see if you can roll housing and enrollment deposits into your financial aid packages) and make your final college decision in time to submit/confirm your deposit at your chosen institution by the May 1 national deposit deadline.
	  ◊ Meet notification deadlines
	  ◊ Do NOT double confirm (there are consequences to this)
	  ◊ Notify other schools that have accepted you if and when you've chosen to deposit at another school (see the following notes on how to frame that email or phone conversation)

When	What to Do

Spring Semester Senior Year	• If you have decided not to attend a school or accept a scholarship, contact them directly and right away. Don't leave them to hear it from their intern, who found out on Facebook. (True story.) Contacting organizations directly shows consideration for other applicants who may be notified of available positions or scholarships once you decline them. You never know when your paths may cross again!
	◊ Again, starting with your interest in their institution or scholarship will serve you well. You can just state that and/or add a line about something specific that you appreciate about their school or organization.
	◊ Thank them for their offer of acceptance, time taken to review your application and/or to interview you. If there is something in particular that struck you positively about your interaction with the organization, feel free to mention it here.
	◊ Let them know that after much thought, you've decided to decline their offer in order
	  - to attend a different school (and let them know which one and why) or
	  - to pursue goals for which the scholarship couldn't be used (please let them know which ones – for example, declining an in-state scholarship to attend a specific school that offers a particular degree you've decided to pursue).
	◊ Close by
	  - saying you wanted to let them know right away in the hopes that another student could benefit in your place
	  - thanking them for their consideration.
	• Send thank you notes to the people who helped you throughout this process. Let them know which school you've selected and which scholarships you've earned.
	• Ask your high school counseling office to send your final transcript to your chosen institution.

2. DON'T FREAK OUT

Are college and scholarship applications basically the same thing?

Some people say yes: scholarship and college applications are essentially the same animal. Another school of thought holds that college applications are more about why you are a good institutional fit, while scholarship applications are more about expressing who you are as a person. But here's the thing: why you are – or aren't – a good institutional fit is because of who you are as a person.

So here's a more useful – and efficient – way of thinking of the different applications:
- Some (like most college applications) are looking for insight into all of you – your academics, your participation and leadership in extracurricular activities, your service work and character, as well as your background and future aspirations.
- Other applications are looking for insight into part of you, such as those for academic scholarships or for admission to collegiate leadership programs.

The truth is that they overlap. Those individual aspects of who you are that specific applications usually center around (such as academics, leadership, or service) are typically included in the applications looking for insight into *all* of you. So, for an application for a leadership program, take the short-answer response you wrote for your college application about the time you most made a difference in the life of another by exercising leadership and expand on it. Or do it the other way around: look at a full application dedicated to one aspect of who you are and pick the short-answer response you like best to use in your application for that full-ride scholarship that's evaluating you as a whole person.

Once you learn how to tackle an application in general, you won't be endlessly creating applications from scratch and you won't have to learn new rules for each one you encounter. So don't freak out – college and scholarship applications are essentially the same thing.

The Common App is Great – and So Are Institutional Applications

You've likely heard of the Common App. Almost 700 colleges and universities accept this standard application, and more are reportedly looking to adopt it in the next few years. This is great news if you're looking to apply to a number of different schools because you can fill out the Common App and then submit it to any of the schools on your list that accept it. For some institutions, that might be it. For others, you might have one or two supplementary sections to fill out. Either way, you won't be repeating the information that all schools definitely want (such as your biographical, family, and academic information).

You also have the option of filling out individual college and university applications, and for schools that don't accept the Common App, you'll have to. Again, don't freak out: these are still basically the same thing. Most schools use applications that ask for the following information, usually in this order:

- Biographical information (your name, school, address, basic information on family and future plans)
- Academic information (your grades, test scores, current class schedule and perhaps a transcript)
- Activities (your involvement in academic, athletic and arts organizations; community service involvements; and work. You may also have a Detailed Activity portion, which we will talk about at the end of the next chapter)
- Short-answer questions (mini essays that are typically focused on individual selection criteria)
- The application essay
- Letters of recommendation (which are sometimes requested at the time of submitting your application, and sometimes after you've moved past the preliminary round of selection)

So, again, good news. Even if one of your schools doesn't accept the Common App, you can still re-purpose your responses for the Common App in order to complete the institutional application.

And what if the schools on your list do accept the Common App, but also have their own? If you know you're applying to a number of schools – say, 10 or so – then use the Common App. You'll benefit from not repeating the standard information 10 times on 10 individual applications. If you're just applying to a couple schools, use the institutional applications. Why? Because the institutional applications don't require an account and are sometimes more straightforward than the Common App, and because the institutions can help you more directly if you run into any technical glitches.

The bottom line: most colleges and universities don't have a preference for either their institutional application or the Common App. They just want you to apply. That said, your school counselor or college access advisor might be able to offer some additional insight into what could be best in your particular situation, so check with him or her, too.

You Can – And Should – Reuse Parts of Your Application

Given the above discussion, you know we're in favor of your reusing parts of your applications for multiple institutions. Now, this is something you've probably been warned against by at least one well-meaning adult in your life, and for good reason: there are great ways to do this, and tragic ways to do this. That's something we'll get to in Section 1 of Chapter IV.

Help, and Money, Are Out There

It can be confusing and overwhelming to think about applying and paying for college, but there are resources to help you. In addition to leaning on the teachers, counselors, coaches and other people in your life (more on this later), there are a number of online resources to help you understand the process of college admission and to find money to pay for it. Or, better yet, check out the resources with some of the people in your corner to ensure you're getting the most out of the information that the web can provide.

There are also scams online that you need to watch out for, so as a rule, don't pay money for any information online. Instead, look for resources from these trusted sources and gather information directly from the institutions to which you are applying. Since specific links can change, we've primarily listed the names of the organizations and whose websites will be particularly useful for you to search.

- **ACT** – The ACT website provides information on the ACT exam, including registration, test prep and scores, as well as dates, practice tests and financial aid.
- **The College Board** - The College Board provides good general information, online registration and test dates for the SAT. In addition, The College Board's Big Future site (search Big Future College Board) is a resource designed with the input of students and educators that makes the college planning process easier to navigate.
- **Consumer Financial Protection Bureau** – Their Paying for College tool allows students to compare all sorts of things, including costs of college, financial aid and loan repayment options.
- **Federal Reserve Bank of San Francisco Return on College Investment tool** – If the cost starts to get you down, check out this tool to get a quick estimate on the return you

can get from getting a college education. College graduates earn more throughout their lifetimes than those who don't graduate from college. Use this tool to enter your annual tuition combined with your spending habits in order to see approximately when you can expect to break even and what return you'll have at different points in your life.

- **FinAid** – The student information, advice and tools on this website include a way to estimate your EFC (Estimated Family Contribution) now to plan ahead financially. It also features links to the scholarship searches listed above, links to colleges' financial aid pages, student loan information and much more.

- **Free Application for Federal Student Aid** (FAFSA – found at www.fafsa.gov rather than one of the fraudulent sites that have been set up in recent years) – All colleges and universities require their students to fill out the FAFSA to be considered for financial aid. You can complete an application at your own pace on the internet and can easily check the status of it later. You can also find information about other financial aid programs on the FAFSA website.

- **Free scholarship searches and resources** – While numerous companies offer scholarship search services for a fee, you can find all of the same information yourself with a little bit of work. Some good places to start searching are: Naviance (if your high school uses it), Scholarship Experts, Princeton Review, Scholarships.com, College Answer, Fastweb and Mach25.

- **National Association of Student Financial Aid Administrators** (NASFAA) – In particular, take a look at their Student Aid Tips for Unique Student Populations, which has targeted advice for undocumented students, wards of the court, foster youth and other underrepresented students.

- **National College Access Network's Form Your Future Campaign** – Most students are eligible for federal financial aid. Go straight to the source and check out information from the Form Your Future Campaign that explains the financial aid process to people advising students.

- **Sallie Mae** – This website presents good general information, a general step-by-step financial aid application process explanation and good information on student loans.

- **The U.S. Department of Education** – The Department of Ed has an online Financial Aid Toolkit that your school counselor and people working with college access programs will know well. Its website also features information on Federal Student Aid (FSA) programs, including how to apply and receive funding, as well as information on maximum awards and eligibility.

NOTE: Don't let the price of a school keep you from applying. Many students get financial aid, which can make schools that appear more expensive more affordable. That said, it's a good idea to apply to 3-7 schools if you can, with a couple being schools where your grades and test scores are quite a bit above the schools' averages, a couple more where your grades and test scores are the same as the schools' averages, and a couple reach schools, whose averages are well above your grades and test scores. Then you can wait to see where you're accepted and what your financial aid packages look like before making a decision about which overall package is the best choice for you. Remember, too, that many institutions offer application fee waivers for those experiencing economic hardship in order to keep accumulating fees from preventing students from applying to multiple schools.

Dips in Grades, Declining Extracurricular Participation and Poor Decisions Can be Explained

We're often asked by counselors, parents and students if it's best to address dips in grades and participation in the application. While it might be tempting to avoid calling attention to those times when you feel you weren't performing your best, reviewers understand that sometimes life gets in the way. You are usually better off addressing the issue head-on.

Getting B's for a semester doesn't need to be explained, but if you have two years of straight A's followed by a semester of D's or F's, that's going to raise a red flag for any reviewer looking over your transcript. You could leave the application reader to fill in the blanks (perhaps assuming the worst), or you could make a note about what particular life circumstances you were facing that resulted in the decreased performance. Good places to address this include the essay, short answer questions, or any area for special or extenuating circumstances.

You don't need to dwell on it. Just address the situation and what contributed to it (examples: a death in the family, a move across the country, your parents divorced, and so on). Ideally, the semester following the life event will show your participation and academic performance getting back to the level it was before misfortune struck. If so, indicate that in your explanation. If not, mention what you're doing now to get back on track (such as seeing a counselor or tutor).

A related issue is addressing lapses in judgment that have resulted in disciplinary action at the school or local level. This is admittedly a fine line to walk. It's also possible that such an experience may well have been one of the most educational in your life. We would encourage you to talk with your people (see section four of this chapter for whom we mean by that) and to draft an essay about such life experiences to see if it's something that you think will add to your application. Did what you learned lead you to new heights of self-awareness and maturity? Then include it. Do you feel its inclusion will do you more harm than good? Then it's fine to omit. Just be aware that reviewers may learn of the incident by other means, such as letters of recommendation, reviewers at other institutions or programs, or even neighbors or social media. **As a rule, it's better to control your message rather than leaving it up to chance.**

People Can and Will Help You

Again, section four of this chapter provides detailed information on how to identify and rally the people in your life. Also feel free to call admissions representatives at the colleges and universities to which you're applying or program officers at scholarship providers if you have any questions you can't answer by reading the instructions on the applications, looking at their websites, or referring to correspondence from the organizations. We've offered tips for how to structure these communications in the table included in Chapter III, section 1 under actions to take in spring semester of junior year.

Many students are reluctant to reach out to these professionals for fear of looking stupid. Yet think of it from their point of view: program and admission officers spend a lot of time doing paperwork, working with spreadsheets, and reading about conscientious, interesting people. Don't you think they'd rather talk to these people? If you've reviewed the materials you have from the organization, your question will be thoughtful. We trust that you'll be courteous on the phone and grateful for any additional information you receive, ensuring that the person you talk to will have been genuinely happy to speak with you.

Consistency is Key

We were recently at a conference for high school and college admission counselors where an entire panel of speakers groaned audibly when one of them grumbled about having to give this piece of advice: use your full name and the same name on everything you do: your transcripts, your test scores, your applications for institutions and for scholarships. Be mindful that if you're a U.S. resident and have filled out the FAFSA (as we strongly recommend that you do in the fall of your senior year), the name you use on all of your applications should be the same one that's on your social security card. Otherwise, some institutional systems will generate duplicate records for you – one with the name you used on your application to the institution, and one for the name you used on your FAFSA, which mirrors the name listed on your social security card.

And use the same, professional email, too (no SugarBunny@xyz.com). A simple email, featuring your first and last name, as well as making sure you use the same name on all of your materials, will help program officers and admission counselors connect everything. That ensures that your application package is complete and accurate as quickly as possible, which means you may be notified of your status in their selection process more quickly. If college admissions directors get visibly annoyed by students who aren't consistent in this way, it seems like something you might want to avoid.

On a similar note, if you've already started an application – be it an institutional application or the Common App – you need to stick with that type of application. Many students will start one application, stop, and then start again on a second. This can cause a lot of processing errors, and processing errors don't work in your favor.

Be Responsive

Remember that simple, professional email account we mentioned? Check it. Regularly. And that includes your SPAM filter or junk folder. What is regularly? Every 48 hours, for starters, and also whenever you're specifically expecting correspondence from organizations (such as their scholarship semifinalist notification deadline). Institutional representatives find it incredibly irritating to hear students complain that they haven't received materials, only to realize that they created a new email address for their application process and forgot to check it.

You may also want to know that we can see when – or if – you open your messages. If we sent you a message asking you to invite your recommenders to log in to our letter of recommendation site, and we've specifically asked you to do this as soon as possible in order to be respectful of their time, do so. It means something —and not in a good way — if you don't.

3. WHICH DEADLINES ARE BINDING OR NON-BINDING, AND WHICH SHOULD YOU CHOOSE?

If you've heard of binding and non-binding deadlines, you know that there are different ways to apply to colleges that pledge you to restricting your actions in exchange for what is seen as slight advantages in the application process.

By applying through Early Decision, for example, you are committing to attend that university if you are accepted. This is, on its surface, a way for a student to show the institution that he or she is particularly interested in that school – that it's his or her top choice – and therefore to raise that student's application in the eyes of the school (so long as he or she is qualified). Admissions reps gain more certainty in knowing that an acceptance won't go to waste on a student applying through Early Decision because that student has committed to enrolling should he or she be accepted, and so won't decline, leaving the school with an empty spot to fill late in the admission process after already notifying other students. The disadvantage of this, however, is the binding part. That means you're obligated to go to that school even if you've found a better fit elsewhere (which includes a better financial fit).

NOTE: it's true that colleges and universities can't enforce this contract by law, but they do take it very seriously. We've heard stories from our admission office colleagues of getting calls from other institutions where students had applied early decision and broken their commitments in order to go to that representative's institution. The students likely thought they were gaming the system, applying to two schools through the binding Early Decision process. But by not honoring that binding agreement, they shot themselves in the foot because the school they withdrew from called the one they hoped to enroll at…and that chosen school decided to revoke their offer of acceptance due to concerns about the students' integrity. So make no mistake, if you apply Early Decision, you should be certain that you'll enroll at that institution.

Because of this, we *generally* recommend that students apply through non-binding Early Action or Rolling Decision/Regular Decision processes in order to keep options open. That said, you may be in a particular situation that leads you to consider one of the other options. Charts like the one below are widely available online to help discern the difference between common terms used in the application process in order to make the best choice for you.

Non-Binding Application Processes: students are free to apply to other institutions and have until the May 1 national deposit deadline to confirm enrollment at their chosen school	
Rolling Decision	Institutions review applications as they are received and make their decisions as to whether to admit those students on an on-going basis throughout the application cycle.
Regular Decision	Institutions state a clear deadline for student applications and a clear time span in which they will receive news of their admission status.
Early Action (EA)	In exchange for receiving student applications early (usually between October and December), institutions promise to notify applicants of their admission status well before the institutions' regular response date (this advance notification period usually spans from December to February). There is no harm in applying Early Action; in fact, it could be preferable to applying late in the application cycle when freshmen classes start to fill at selective institutions.

Binding Application Processes: restrictions that students are responsible for understanding and following are placed on student activity (see below)	
Early Decision (ED)	Described above, this is the process through which students make a commitment to their top choice school, promising to enroll there if they are admitted and given enough financial aid. Students may also apply to other schools through Regular Admission, but if accepted to their Early Decision school, they are expected to withdraw those other applications in favor of their Early Decision school. Only apply Early Decision if you a) have one clear top-choice school where you want to increase your likelihood of acceptance b) know you'll get enough financial aid or loans to cover the cost of attendance and c) understand you cannot break your commitment to attend the institution if accepted.
Restrictive Early Action (REA)	Through this process, students can only apply to one school early (so certainly not multiple via Early Decision or Restrictive Early Action, but also not multiple schools through Early Action). Students may also apply to other schools through Regular Admission, and, if accepted to their Restrictive Early Action school, they have until early spring to give that school their final decision. While less restrictive than Early Decision, Restrictive Early Action still narrows students' options.

4. CALL ON YOUR PEOPLE: YOUR COMMUNITY WANTS TO HELP YOU

Think about the people you've always known to be in your corner—the ones you can count on for anything, whose house you find yourself headed toward at the end of a bad day, whose phone number is in your favorites. Then consider how these people—parents, friends, teachers, your current or former boss, counselors, college access advisors, coaches, club sponsors, religious and community leaders, older siblings—can help you take the application process by storm.

The students who earn our full-ride scholarships consistently tell us that they've called on their personal pit crews to check for blind spots and amplify their impact. Leaning on the people who know them well, students receive valuable advice and stellar letters of recommendation that help their applications stand out.

We know it takes courage to ask people to help you, especially on something that can be incredibly personal, like writing in detail about your life in order to represent yourself in a college or scholarship application. Yet taking the personal risk of being vulnerable enough to ask for help and then giving yourself permission to really receive that help can be the most important step toward fulfilling your dreams – both of college and of life after college. And remember: it's not strange that you might need help! By definition, high school seniors have never applied for college. People will expect you to have questions, and when you do, here are some good types of people to ask:

- Your high school counselor and/or college access advisor – these people are skilled in the college and scholarship application processes, and are likely to have personal and professional relationships with college admission counselors
- Your English teacher and/or newspaper/yearbook/literary journal advisor – Those with skill in writing can help you organize your thoughts, proofread your essays and write compelling letters of recommendation
- Older friends, siblings or cousins – These people can be particularly helpful if they are in or have gone to college because they can share their own experiences. But even if they haven't enrolled in college themselves, they will know you well and may also have experience with resumes and interviews through their work experience, all of which can be helpful.

- Parents/guardians, aunts, uncles, grandparents, coaches, spiritual leaders, mentors, etc. – Similar to the above, the adults in your life know you well, which is invaluable in the college and scholarship application process. Even if they haven't been to college and are stumped by the FAFSA (as most of us are when we first look at it), these adults in your life can go with you to meet your guidance counselor and/or college access advisor or look through online resources with you to help make sense of it all. As great as people your own age are for providing support, adults often have more knowledge simply because of their additional life experience. If they don't know the answer, they may be able to connect you with the right person or resource to find the answers you need.

There are also a number of organizations specifically dedicated to helping students who want to go to college. Here's a list of places to look up online in order to find support near you:

- **College Greenlight** – A site designed to connect first-generation and underrepresented students to colleges and scholarships, as well as counselors and mentors.
- **The Council for Opportunity in Education directory of TRIO and GEAR UP programs** – This directory provides a comprehensive list of programs designed to help low-income students enroll in and graduate from college.
- **I'm First!** – This online community for first-generation college students and the people who support them connects you with advice from currently enrolled first-gen students and provides tips, reminders, Google+ Hangouts, Twitter chats and other ways of answering common questions about the admission process.
- **KnowHow2Go** – The American Council on Education, Lumina Foundation and the Ad Council created this campaign specifically to help low-income and first generation college students with the college process. Their website provides lots of advice, as well as the opportunity to search for local resources
- **National College Access Network** – Reviewing this website can point you to more than 400 organizations that are members of this network and are located nationwide.
- **The National Partnership for Education** – Organizations that are members of this partnership serve under-represented students applying for and attending college. There are more than 300 organizations in the partnership, located in almost 35 states.

While each student's support crew is as different as they are, everyone has a couple people who want to do anything they can to help that student pursue his or her goals. That's why many people become teachers, coaches and religious leaders who work with young adults – because they want to help students discover their strengths, passions and ambitions in order to lead fulfilling, successful lives. As you read through the targeted strategies in this book, ask yourself at each stage, "Who can take my work to the next level? Who can help me keep focused and energized and make the most of my time on both college and scholarship applications?" Planning who you will ask for which type of assistance ahead of time will ensure that you receive different viewpoints.

Appropriate things to ask a variety of people to help you with are:
- Finding scholarships. Your high school guidance counselor and/or college access advisor will be the best person to turn to first for this advice. Even if you don't know him or her well, your counselor/advisor will be happy to help. Counselors consistently tell us that supporting students in pursuing their dreams is one of their favorite parts of their jobs (far more so than facilitating schedule changes)! Also check out national websites such as those listed in section one of this chapter.
- Deciding on the colleges and universities you want to apply to, and considering how you'll rank them in order of which is the best fit for you.
- Reviewing FAFSA and CSS Profile applications.
- Reviewing the activity section of your application. Ask your people to make sure that you didn't forget any activities, accomplishments or contributions. People who know you can also make sure that you are not being overly humble or confident in your written descriptions. (See section three of Chapter IV for more about this.)
- Helping you choose an essay topic and/or reading a variety of drafted essays to help you choose the best one.
- Editing various drafts of your essay and/or short answer responses to make them the best they can be.
- Preparing for your interview.

A word of caution here: don't cross the line. While calling on your people brings you invaluable feedback, don't ever allow any of them to write any portion of your application for you, even if they try to insist. It doesn't make you look good, it's a poor habit to get into, and—most importantly—we can tell. How? Let us count the ways:
1. The application uses second-person "she/he" or the student's name instead of the first-person "I." (Seriously.)
2. The application gives itself away by using an inappropriate verb tense. For example, the student may think to take out his or her name and substitute an "I," but then forgets to alter the verb tense—so that "[Student] runs on the track team" becomes "I runs on the track team." Clever, but not clever enough.

3. The application features dated words/expressions. Few 17-year-olds use terms like "ragamuffin," "kit and caboodle" or "world wide web."

4. A parent calls with questions all the time and says "I" or "we" when framing those questions, rather than conveying what the student wants to know.

5. Different parts of the application sound like they were written by different people because they're so inconsistent in tone, level of formality, syntax or length.

6. The student doesn't seem at all familiar with his or her own application at the interview.

7. The application includes details about random childhood accomplishments from a parent's perspective—for instance, "Ever since I led the annual Independence Day parade as a toddler, adorably perched atop the town's fire truck..."

8. The application describes student activities such as National Honor Society and Key Club with generic information cut and pasted from national websites.

IV. OVERALL COMMENTS THAT APPLY TO THE WHOLE APPLICATION

1. STRATEGIES FOR REUSING PARTS OF PREVIOUS APPLICATIONS

Here's a secret: Application reviewers don't want to waste your time any more than we want you to waste ours. We are all looking for the best candidates to attend our institutions or earn our scholarships, and the best way to do that is to evaluate your best work. But we can't do that if you've already sent your best work to someone else and feel like you have to crank out something new for us, even if it's mediocre.

We also know that your best work takes time. We don't want you to burn that time trying to perfect a second-rate essay. And we don't want to read a second-rate essay.

Make the Most of Your Time

The vast majority of colleges and scholarship providers are asking for the same things:
- Detailed information on the activities you've participated in during high school, both in your school and your community
- Academic information
- Responses to short-answer questions
- A personal essay
- Letters of recommendation
- An admissions interview (not always, but often)

This means that you can mix and match various application components for different institutions, tailoring them for the different organizations' selection criteria, which we'll tell you more about in each section of this book.

Make People Feel Special

Application reviewers are only human. We want to feel special. We want to feel like you know us and chose to apply for our particular scholarship or institution. Clearly, there was some choice on your part, even though we know that you're applying to several organizations simultaneously. We just don't want you to hit us over the head with that fact by referring to another college in the essay you submit to us, or by saying you've always dreamed of earning X scholarship…when we work for Y.

So once you've given yourself enough time to make the basic components of your application the best they can possibly be, follow these strategies to make sure that your best work feels new and is personalized to each organization you address:

- **Read every word** of each section after you've copied and pasted to ensure that you have not referenced another institution or organization by mistake. Remind the people who are writing your letters of recommendation about this, too. Also, be careful when calling or emailing colleges and scholarship providers not to refer to them as members of other institutions. We do remember you once you've called.

- **Avoid generalities** that scream "form letter," such as "if admitted to your institution" or "if chosen for your scholarship." Replace each reference with a specific institution's or scholarship's name.

- **Highlight the things that particular scholarship or organization is looking for,** such as community service or in-state school attendance. And, when possible, use a specific phrase or two to highlight this. Maybe one school seeks students with "intellectual curiosity" while another says it's looking for candidates interested in "living a life of the mind." Both mean essentially the same thing, and using one phrase with a different organization won't get you in trouble. But it never hurts to show that you have been paying attention to exactly what they want.

- **If you're reusing an essay or short-answer response, make sure that it directly and completely addresses the new prompt.** Sometimes you'll need to add or subtract a paragraph to show that you know how to follow directions and to make it appear as if you wrote the recycled essay for that new application alone.

- **Make sure you are not copying and pasting error**s—for example, that your essay or short answer response is missing the first sentence, or that there are random font changes.

- **Similarly, whenever possible, insert a phrase or two that shows you're familiar with the institution.** For example, our foundation was created by the Boettcher family, Prussian immigrants who earned their wealth through operating hardware businesses during the silver boom, introducing the sugar beet industry in Colorado, and producing cement for the western United States, among other entrepreneurial ventures. Mentioning a bit of history easily found on our website isn't going to earn somebody a scholarship all by itself, but it does show the applicant cares enough about our organization to have done a little homework.

2. NAIL THE BASICS THAT MANY OTHERS FORGET

You may think the following reminders would fall under the category of "junk" rather than the wisdom we've promised. We would have thought so, too, if it weren't for the fact that we receive an insane number of applications every year that forget to do these exact same things. Reviewers for many selection processes will count you out immediately for one of these; others will just grit their teeth and start reading, already annoyed with you. Remember: reviewers are reading piles of applications, front to back, one after the other for days and weeks in a row. Mistake number one for you may be mistake number 100 for them. Don't make yourself the target for the pent-up frustration caused by the 99 who came before you. Specifically:

- **Follow instructions.** Many applications will outline space and length requirements, will tell you if they prefer/accept hard copy applications versus online applications, and will state whether they accept supplemental material such as resumes or news clippings. Read the instructions carefully and pay attention to these specifics when completing your application. The individuals reading your application are often the same people who wrote these instructions. That means they're intimately familiar with them and think they're important. Following the directions shows that you're considerate and that you respect the organization enough to trust they're asking you to fill out the application in a particular way for a good reason (which they are). Do not assume that certain instructions don't apply to you. The classic example of this is when an institution asks for test scores to be sent electronically from the testing agency, and a student doesn't do so because the test scores are printed on his or her high school transcript. Institutions know that test scores are often printed on transcripts; they also know that electronic scores contain more information that can be directly fed into their databases on thousands of students – information that would be a Herculean task to enter by hand for each individual student. It's no accident if an institution asks for something in a specific format. If you feel compelled to know more detail about some specific instruction, call to ask. And while we're talking about instructions, please don't forget to give us all the information we need. For instance, tell us all of your leadership positions, contributions and awards, and answer the entire question/prompt for essays and short answer questions. (See Chapter VII, Section two for information on how to dissect common essay prompts to determine what exactly the committee is looking for.)
- **Meet deadlines.** Plan accordingly and submit your application well before the deadline to leave time for follow-up, if necessary. If others are submitting information on your behalf, such as letters of recommendation or supplemental materials, make sure they also know the

deadlines and follow up with them to make sure their materials are submitted on time. You can also call the institution to ensure receipt of all application components.

Many selection processes also require that standardized test scores be sent directly from SAT or ACT whether hardcopy or electronic. This can take weeks, and also be expensive. To ensure that they arrive on time, know the institution codes for the colleges and scholarship providers to which you will definitely be applying when you sit for the exams (you can find these on the ACT and SAT websites and/or by asking your high school counselor or college access advisor for help). List as many codes as you can when you fill out the preliminary test information, then request any needed additional reports right after. In addition to ensuring they arrive in time, this advance planning helps you avoid paying extra to have your score reports rushed to the institution if, in fact, they do require official score reports, as opposed to copies on your transcript or emailed PDFs.

- **Print a copy of everything** for your records. Many interview questions come from the application, so keeping a copy to review before an interview can be helpful. As you fill out subsequent applications, it can also be helpful to refer to those you have already completed. The other thing is that technology is not always your friend. Sometimes you hit "submit" on an online application just as the server crashes. You may even receive a confirmation report only to find the file was corrupted and not transmitted or received. You might save a document as a PDF file and then find that for some reason you are unable to open it six months later when you sit down to prepare for your interview. The bottom line: there's enough to worry about during this process that you can't control. Do yourself a favor and keep copies of all your application files on your hard drive or jump drive, and in an old-fashioned hard copy. Meanwhile, you won't waste time worrying that you won't be able to access something you need.

- **Proofread.** Seriously. Read every word of the application from start to finish before you submit it. Look, in particular, for places where you may have inadvertently deleted words. Look for words for which you are not 100 percent sure of the definition or that you don't use regularly, and cut or replace them with a synonym you do know and use. Check for typos, words you failed to capitalize correctly and words that the online application software has not accepted, such as those with accents or that are in a language other than English. (For example, did cliché come out as clich? Did your hyphenated word show up as (^:!)?) Reviewers don't expect perfection, just that you will have reviewed your work attentively.

- **Think of your application as a whole.** Committees will read your entire application from front to back in one sitting. You should do that, too – not just to proofread, as mentioned above, but also to make sure that you're maximizing every opportunity offered by the application. You don't need to reiterate what classes you've taken or slip in the fact that you were NHS president multiple times. If you read from the first page to the last, in order, all at once, you can eliminate redundancies and get a sense for what themes will resonate in your application. Your discussion on page six about how much you love music is more believable for your reviewers when they've already seen on pages two through four that you not only participate in four different bands, but also teach piano and organize volunteer recitals at the senior center.

Throughout the reading process, the key is to ask yourself what each section adds to the application in terms of presenting you in your whole, interesting, complicated self. If you find yourself talking about the same thing more than once, ask yourself why. If you're talking about it from a different angle (what Boy Scouts taught you about leadership versus why it's your favorite service activity), then fine. Just make sure that the second reference provides new information and is fresh enough to maintain the reviewer's interest. The exception to this rule is if you've won a national or international award. If you are ranked eighth in the world for Irish Step Dancing, by all means, throw that in there two or three times. Otherwise, once is enough.

Finally, remember that, like a book, your application should present a coherent story about who you are. Make sure you don't contradict yourself, leave holes in the plot or ignore important actors. As reviewers, we don't want to feel disjointed after reading your application. We want a clear picture of the student we're considering for admission or scholarship money. Avoid these mistakes, and you're much more likely to successfully tell your story.

3. SHARE YOUR ACCOMPLISHMENTS WITHOUT SOUNDING ARROGANT

Each year we receive calls from students, parents and counselors wondering why particular applicants have been winnowed out of our selection process. As we walk through the applications in question, we invariably find that these students have either under- or over-stated their contributions. Being too humble can make a leader seem like one who follows the crowd; being too proud can make real contributions seem arrogant—and for our reviewers, arrogance is the number one turn-off.

We've provided the following examples to illustrate the right chord to strike in your application: the straightforward or factual tone.

Section A provides three ways of describing involvement in the activities section of the application. Notice how neither the overly humble nor overly proud versions of telling the same story serve the student as well as the straightforward one.

Section B drills down into specific phrasing for short answer questions about a variety of activities that could be shielding actual contributions or overstating them in a way that could turn off reviewers, plus one example that takes the middle path.

Section C provides examples of full essays that struck our committee members as particularly meek, arrogant or suitably straightforward – and our comments as to why.

Section A - Detailed Activity List Examples

The examples below describe a hypothetical applicant's involvement in the same activity using three different tones. Take a look at our reviewers' responses and comments to each example.

Example 1: Overly Humble

Name of Organization	Key Club
Year	9 ☐ 10 ☒ 11 ☒ 12 ☒
Hrs/wk	5
Wks/yr	34
Sponsor's Name	Mr. Thomas Greene
Leadership Positions Held	Co-President
Honors or Awards	
Personal Contributions:	I participated in the school chapter of the Key Club, which completed over 1300 cumulative hours of service. We started a new food drive that collected produce from backyard gardens for the food bank. We also went caroling at the Alzheimer's unit at the nursing home down the street, and invited the school choir to perform a holiday concert for the residents.

This could be appropriate if it was truly a group effort, but from the factual example below, it's clear the student led this event.

As Co-President, "participated" certainly understates his leadership role.

While the student surely participated, it's even more impressive that he directed the effort, as seen in the factual example.

Example 2: Overly Proud/Arrogant

Name of Organization	Key Club
Year	9 ☐ 10 ☒ 11 ☒ 12 ☒
Hrs/wk	5
Wks/yr	34
Sponsor's Name	Mr. Thomas Greene
Leadership Positions Held	Co-President
Honors or Awards	Best School Club (Yearbook), National Key Club Participation Award
Personal Contributions:	I was president of the Key Club, and oversaw the completion of 1300 cumulative hours of service—the most in school history. I collected over 900 pounds of food through my "Harvest Food Drive" initiative. Last but not least, I singlehandedly organized caroling at the assisted living community down the street, and invited the school choir to perform a concert for the residents. Finally, I received national recognition for community impact.

We see from the title listed above that the student was Co-President. This is either overstating or failing to tell a story about how the other Co-President flaked.

"oversaw" implies direct supervision, which seems unlikely. That, coupled with "the most in school history" seems a bit much.

This is fine, but not as important as the other award.

Ick. It just sounds like he is impressed with himself. Did NO ONE help? If no one did, listing what his accomplishment was could still be presented in a way that was more factual and less self-absorbed.

Ick again: The club had community impact and he took credit.

Example 3: Straightforward/Factual

Name of Organization	Key Club
Year	9 ☐ 10 ☒ 11 ☒ 12 ☒
Hrs/wk	5
Wks/yr	34
Sponsor's Name	Mr. Thomas Greene
Leadership Positions Held	Co-President
Honors or Awards	National Key Club Participation Award
Personal Contributions:	As co-president of Key Club, I helped students complete over 1300 cumulative hours of service. I spearheaded a "Harvest Food Drive" that collected over 900 pounds of food from backyard gardens for the Golden Food Bank. I also organized caroling at a nearby nursing home and invited the school choir to perform their holiday concert for the residents.

This is important! Don't be shy about recognition or awards.

1300 hours and 900 lbs. of food—these are great ways to quantify your impact. Sure, the student didn't do all this alone, but if he hadn't initiated the food drive, nothing would have been collected.

If "spearheaded" makes you uncomfortable, "led" or "directed" would work just as well. The key is to honestly own your contributions.

Shows initiative that isn't captured in the "overly humble" example above

Section B – Short Essay Response Examples

The examples below are from actual applications. While they discuss different activities, their relative tones – and the impact of them – are apparent.

Example 1: Overly Humble

"Select your favorite service activity, and describe why it is important to you and your community."

"Helped assist in running, or "helped run?" The second option is stronger and likely still accurate.

In talking with the student we learned that she DESIGNED them independently from start to finish. "Assist in designing" is not nearly as strong – or accurate – as "design."

My favorite service activity is the volunteer work I do at an after school enrichment program at the elementary school. For a few years, I have helped assist the volunteer coordinator of our school in running the program by completing a number of tasks. I assist in designing lesson plans and games, and welcome new students. I love this volunteer work because of the enormous difference the program makes in the lives of the students. The program helps kindergarteners and low-income students meet friends and develop self-confidence. Although the work I do isn't that important, an official "Find a Friend Program" has been made, whose purpose is to make sure that all students are paired with a buddy if they just go to a spot on the playground that's painted on the ground with "I could use a friend" printed around the colored circle. A few of the less popular students have been welcomed into the class, and I hope they feel a sense confidence that will follow them wherever they go.

One sentence about the program's impact is good – she should then use the second sentence to state how her impact allows the program to be even more effective.

Of course it is!

Did this student create the "Find a Friend Program?" Passive voice can often indicate that a student has left her role out. Who made the program? How did it just "get made?"

In general, this description focuses more on the other students than the applicant's role, which is fine so long as the applicant's contributions aren't totally hidden as a result. Give us some personal pronouns (I, me, my) and action verbs (ran, started, supported) that convey the scope and impact of your involvement.

Example 2: Overly Proud/Arrogant

"Describe a specific situation or activity in which you made a difference in the lives of others through your effectiveness as a leader."

Ick! Striking "my defeated competitors clapping for me" would convey the same accomplishment without the insensitivity and poor sportsmanship.

As I stood on the podium, my defeated competitors clapping for me, my parents smiling, I knew that I had achieved my dream. I had won the KLC Cup.

Last year, my tennis doubles team won the regional championship and earned a spot at the KLC Cup state tournament. Although my partner and I had always been treated as equals, in our last practice before the tournament, the training manager announced that I should lead the team as captain. He informed me that I was the powerhouse player for the club, and that with great power, comes great responsibility. I was going to have to encourage my doubles partner, as well as all the other teams, even though I knew they were going to lose.

At first, the tournament did not go according to plan. Due to a number of mistakes by my partner and a missed serve on my part, we lost our first match to an inferior team. My whole training club was discouraged, and I was too, but I managed to carry us through. In the next match, I stepped out on the court determined to win, and I did. All the other teams we knocked out in the first round like I predicted, but I had to win to give them hope. And win I did.

My partner and I finished tournament in first place, and I was tournament MVP. Even though the other teams weren't at the same caliber, they at least were awarded the sportsmanship award to feel better about themselves. Marching up to the stage to receive the KLC Cup, I knew I had led my team to victory.

Example 3: Straightforward/Factual

"Pick one thing you really enjoy and tell us why you love it."

Standing in front of crowd, slight butterflies in my stomach, microphone in hand or not, I'm ready. I love speaking in front of people, and have won a number of awards for talking about what's important to me and serving as a voice for others. I've always had a knack for being able to articulate my thoughts and opinions in an eloquent way when in front of crowd. Whether I am in front of my peers, supporters of my cause, or the opposition, I love presenting my case. When I am speaking publicly, I represent several communities, my local community, my neighborhood and my high school. But I am also a representative of young people, of young women and of Latinas. It is an immense responsibility, but one I feel honored to take on. Before anything, I take into consideration all the people and groups that I represent. I am proud *of the communities I represent and I speak as such. I strive to exude confidence, knowledge, and integrity with every syllable spoken as a means of getting my point across.*

This speaks to the student's core identity. Others might reject or resent the responsibility she feels in representing her various communities – or feel any number of other ways about their position. But for this student, the bottom line is that she speaks in alignment with the pride she feels for her communities.

Section C – Long Essay Response Examples

Example 1: Overly Humble

"Evaluate a significant experience or achievement that has a special meaning to you."

Trying new things can be terrifying, especially thousands of miles away from the comforts of home. I encountered this fear the summer before my junior year, when my church youth group traveled to Colombia over spring break to build homes for single mothers. In addition to pushing our limits of fun and labor, my youth group members and I grew personally and gained a profound appreciation for service abroad by speaking with the families we served.

Our trip represented a number of important milestones in my life. It was the first time I had ever been out of the country, and without the guidance of my parents or a hand to hold on the plane, I had to overcome homesickness. Learning to take care of myself from day one—for example, speaking in Spanish to find my lost luggage in Bogotá, Colombia —was a shock, but a valuable experience. That trip gave me an opportunity that I had never had before: the chance to be truly independent and survive on my own.

The service component and our related activities also gave me insight into myself and my limits. Our group was tasked with building homes for three women and their children in a small village. Since I speak Spanish, I was able to help assist with translation between the pastor and the local congregation that was helping us. In this capacity, I heard the mothers tell unimaginable tragedies about rape, abuse and being exiled by their families. Living day to day, worried about where their children would sleep and what they would eat that night had consumed their hope and their ability to think about the future.

This paragraph tells us some of the "what" – what happened, but not the "so what?" Why was this a valuable experience? What meaning did he derive from it? How did it start him on his journey of growth?

What were these insights? It feels like the student is wary of putting himself in the essay too much when that is the purpose of the application essay.

And how did this hit the student? How did he view his own experience through new eyes, having been exposed to these intimate stories first-hand due to his ability to speak with the women in their own language?

This sentence addresses the impact on the entire group, rather than just the student himself, which doesn't allow us to see him as clearly as we'd like. This is his chance to show up in his own application as an individual apart from any group. Secondarily, it's unlikely that the whole group had the same experience and, even if they did, it's not the student's responsibility to capture everyone's experience—just his. This is both more reasonable and will serve him better.

This is an important role for this student in particular – a chance for him to talk about the difference he made and what he learned about himself as a result. A note on phrasing: "help assist with translation" is not as strong as "helped translate."

Again, this paragraph shifts back to the group as a whole, avoiding the self-reflection and personal contributions that could be featured.

Before departing at the week's end, our group had the opportunity to play with the kids who would inhabit the new homes. Seeing the children smile as they jumped around their new bedrooms brought a smile to all our faces. Even though our impact was small, our youth group was proud that we had changed the lives of a few families and given them hope for the future.

Yet we still haven't seen that because the student is so absent from the essay. What is he doing differently now that he's returned from the trip? How has he changed as an individual?

Many people think of a mission trip as nothing more than a vacation with volunteer work. However, for me, the mission trip to Colombia was a life-changing experience. Although we went to serve the Colombian women, their ability to show us more about ourselves was far greater than our contributions to them. The trip showed us that a child's hopeful smile means so much more than our own money and comfort.

Example 2: Overly Proud/Arrogant

"Evaluate a significant experience or achievement that has a special meaning to you."

Ahh! A paragraph that seems to start out revering a time-honored instructor turns into a rhetorical tower built only to put this student at the top of it. The thrust of the paragraph is "I am a crazy brilliant student who excelled in the one class that rises above all others in prestige and intellectual challenge."

At my high school, one class rises above the rest in prestige and intellectual challenge: AP Physics taught by Dr. Matthews, a great physicist who used to teach at Oxford. I have to say, the students who weren't meant for such a hard class just have to drop out, but the decent ones push through. The crazy brilliant ones excel in the course, and take Statistical Mechanics at college in the spring. I'm one of those students.

Ouch. Attitude.

Since I excelled in Advanced Physics and Calculus, I didn't think AP Physics would be much more than a bore. However, I discovered how math can morph from easy concepts like density and the Copernican Principle into quantum theory and the Uncertainty Principle. I've spent more time on this class than all of my other classes. Don't get me wrong, I think the class is just the right thing for students like me, but I think Dr. Matthews sets the bar even higher for me because he knows what I'm capable of.

Again, this comes across as the student thinking she's better than others in the class. Maybe this is because she's cut herself off before explaining her close relationship with the teacher or why she needed extra challenge/pushing; but, whatever the reason, the result is probably not helping her.

This wording seems to lead to unintentionally disclosing that the student usually doesn't try too hard, caring more about the grades than the learning. It also, in the second sentence, ties itself into knots by making a statement only to immediately undercut it just a few words later. Our guess is that this comes from being so focused on making herself look good rather than just telling her story.

Due to this high bar I've learned so much. Usually, I was able to turn assignments in at the last minute and get 100 percent, but I've learned that procrastination doesn't work for this class. I'm used to producing complicated and intelligent work, but Dr. Matthews really demands quality work (not to say that I ever produced poor quality work). What

I've learned the most is about AP Physics, and although I struggled at first, I've been acing my exams and plan to compete in a regional science tournament next spring.

My most proud moment was earlier this year, however, when I picked up the school newspaper. I noticed that one of my regional science prizes had been featured in the newspaper. This meant even more to me than all my perfect scores and a perfect ACT. Greatness is expected of me, but a simple act of recognition like that made my day. Seeing my prize in the newspaper meant that I had lived up to Dr. Matthews' standards.

I never expected to be in the newspaper, but it happened anyway. It just goes to show the students who couldn't handle AP Physics that doing well on every assignment does pay off.

This is a confusing and off-topic paragraph that seems inserted merely to list a number of accolades the student wants to brag about. More interesting – and revelatory – would be to hear about the bumpy path to her learning she couldn't just turn in assignments at the last minute – and what else she confronted – to do well in the class.

This is unnecessary – the student would serve herself better if she focused on her own accomplishments rather than putting others down.

Example 3: Straightforward/Factual

"Describe a person who has had a significant influence on you and discuss his or her influence."

I will never forget the night last year I was woken up at 3am by the loud bangs and screams coming from downstairs. I jumped out of bed and ran to the noise to see my mother in the middle of my two older brothers, trying to stop them from engaging in a drunken fight. My mom and I couldn't stop them and I knew I had to call my dad to come home from work to help. When my dad came home, I heard him say the words that changed my life. "I'm battling cancer." Immediately my heart sank and the tears began welling up in my eyes. I fell to my knees at the edge of my parent's bed and completely broke. Everything I had always feared was finally a reality and I didn't know how to control it. I cried until it was time to go to school to take my final exam.

Sharing this picture of fear and sadness in her application takes real courage. It also shows the student's humanity and compassion. We don't know that any of us really knows what to do in a moment like this, and the student's honesty about feeling out of control is moving.

Her willingness to be vulnerable and share these details gives readers insight into her everyday reality, while also showing that the earlier line "everything I had always feared was finally a reality" is very true – not the exaggeration or cliché that others might employ for effect.

Ever since I can remember, my dad has always been sick. At times it was to the point when he couldn't even walk. I was always terrified that I was going to lose him. I would picture my wedding and cry because he may not make it to walk me down the aisle. Every nightmare I have had has been of losing my dad, but thankfully he is still here with me today.

Clearly, this student is not trying to shove a social accomplishment into her essay like we've seen others do. She has done such a good job focusing on the specific characteristics of her dad that she admires, as well as sharing information about his illness, that we understand her reason for mentioning Homecoming here. This was a meaningful accomplishment for her…and her dad understood that, putting personal comfort aside to be there for her.

My father embodies the meaning of strength. He models perseverance and selflessness, and teaches me to push through what life throws at me. NO matter how sick he was, he refused to give up. HE continues to work, providing for our family. Regardless of his health, he offers me unconditional support and has never missed a single softball or soccer game of mine. I'll always remember when he pushed through the pain to walk me down the football field when I won Homecoming Queen. Quitting has never been in his vocabulary. My gratitude pushes me to be like him. I am so blessed to have a father like him. I cherish every lesson he gives me. Every lecture. Every piece of advice. His monumental influence in my life has given me the drive to be a better person.

Sharing what you're grateful for, what makes you feel lucky or blessed or honored, and/or acknowledging how others have helped you, quickly grounds your story in humility.

These lines, as well as the entire essay, avoid coming off as sentimental because of her straightforward and factual tone. She has a "this is how it is" way of telling her story that rings true and keeps it from seeming like she's playing for sympathy.

He has motivated me to persevere even when there are obstacles in my way. He has not only pushed through illness to succeed, but also stereotypes, financial struggles, and dysfunction within my brothers' lives. He teaches me that nothing comes to you without hard work. Because of these lessons, through perseverance and dedication, I still scored a 96% on my final exam even after I spent the previous 12 hours crying. Through determination, I put the hard work and the effort in to be successful; to pursue my dream of becoming a math teacher, my dream of graduating high school as Valedictorian and my dream of being the first person in my family to go to college.

Again, in a different essay something like this could appear as if the student were bragging. But in this context, it's clear that she credits her dad with instilling in her the drive and work ethic that have led to her success. The test score is included as a specific detail that shows the extreme nature of the day, rather than being used to force in a gold star from the student's transcript.

4. GO WITH YOUR QUIRKS

One of the most fun parts of reading college and scholarship applications is learning about people's quirks. We think people are fascinating, and it's so gratifying to read applications from students who have let their unique identities shine through. Nothing is more compelling than someone owning his or her own space.

We still remember the scholarship applicant who shared how she loved to go all out, singing along with her car radio, and whose friends caught her in the school parking lot one afternoon belting out a song before she returned to class. Or the guy who dressed up as a superhero when he was a kid, affixing his bath towel to his shoulders and alighting from one piece of furniture to another in search of adventure. (See Chapter VI Section 3 for more on these two.) Or the girl who broke her elbow in the middle of the soccer game but continued to play, earning her the nickname of "Elbow" for the rest of her high school career (and into college, since we all started to refer to her that way once she received our scholarship).

Sadly, many students seem to think that these most authentic parts of their personal stories aren't serious or important enough to be included in their college applications. The truth is that embracing your eccentricities is one of the best ways to stand out and to make reviewers want to meet you in person.

You may be thinking to yourself, "I'm not quirky. I'm boring." We're positive this isn't true. To start pondering your own quirks and how they might come to light in the various parts of your application, try the exercises below. After those, read through some real-life examples.

- Ask a handful of friends (or your grandmother) to describe what makes you endearing.
- Write your autobiography tweet-style (140 characters or less). What stands out?
- What fad do you secretly wish had never gone out of style?
- Examine your Facebook photos. What emerges as a common theme or environment?
- Has there been a time that someone called you a dork, a nerd or a geek—and you were proud of that label? Why was that so?
- What do you observe about other people that they don't see in themselves?
- What three songs do you most listen to on iTunes? What are your Pandora or Spotify stations? And what does all of this say about your personality?
- Think about an embarrassing situation and how you reacted. Did you try to cover it up? Play it off? Embrace it by laughing at yourself? What happened as a result?
- What is your all-time favorite costume (Halloween, theater, dress-up)? Why were you so happy to be that character?
- If you could be an expert in anything, what would it be? Why?

Highly Competitive Short-Answer Responses that Highlight Individual Quirks

Example 1:

The specificity of detail not only shows us that this student is intimately familiar with this world, but also places us in it. Her powerful imagery allows us to see—and enjoy—what she does.

— *I love wearing my hair in a hairspray-shellacked bun. I love the smell of Marley board, worn-out pointe shoes and hard work that pervades the studio. I love the people, unapologetically themselves, who congregate backstage. I love pointing and flexing my toes against the barre during warm-up. I love the knot of nervous energy that swells in my stomach — before a show. I love wearing the crown of the regal, vindictive and mysterious Black Swan.*

This tells us something specific about this student. Another person would hate performing for this exact reason.

She explains why she dropped another activity (seen elsewhere in the app) and underscores that ballet really is a priority for her.

When I was little, I loved ballet and performing in every show I could. However, as I got older my onslaught of other activities began to eclipse dancing, and I gave it up for several years. This year—the last year I'd be eligible to audition for a part at my ballet studio—I decided I had to go back to my roots. I elected not to play soccer and thus made room in my life for my inherent dancing queen. Now I can't believe I ever gave up ballet. Dancing gives me the chance to drop everything and be someone else, without any deadlines to meet or to-do lists to complete. I love ballet, and I won't be giving it up again anytime soon.

Self-deprecating reference back to the "mysterious Black Swan" reveals humility and a sense of humor.

Example 2:

I love rap music, in particular, rap that tells a story about real problems and experiences. Through their lyrics, rappers share their stories to help us understand that we are not the only people experiencing difficulties. Rap music helps listeners gather around a common purpose.

This short-answer response, from a female applicant, tackles a relatively rare topic in college applications that is truly meaningful to her. From the opening, she paints a different picture of rap than the misogynistic stereotype that it has often been saddled with, while also speaking to her values of unity and community.

A specific list of types of rap – that she then backs up with specific songs – illustrates both her familiarity the genre and also provides support for her later reference to "the diversity" of rap.

—Rap can be thought-provoking, funny, a way to grieve, a way to express regrets, or a way to question ideas. Hopsin's "Ill Mind of Hopsin 7" is what I turn to when I am questioning religion because the lyrics speak to the difficulty of believing in a higher power. Eminem's "Beautiful" is about stepping into other people's shoes to better understand their struggles. It is a song about perseverance, self-confidence, and perspective and is one I listen to when discouraged. Kendrick Lamar's "Swimming Pools (Drank)" is another song on my playlist, as it strengthens my resolve not to succumb to peer pressure. Because of the diversity of rap, I listen to it for many different purposes: as a way to relieve stress, get energized before softball games, and relax before going to sleep. Rap music often gets a bad rap, but I could not imagine my life without it.

These examples are powerful because of how they influence her life. This student doesn't just love rap, she integrates it into her desire to live an examined life…and gives us a glimpse into those reflections here.

Allows us to picture the student – particularly listening to rap in order to "relax before going to sleep." This pastime is unique, endearing and memorable.

Example 3:

Titles aren't necessary, but they can also convey unbridled enthusiasm. This sums up her essay and passion.

— England is Amazing!

I've never been to England, but I love it. There's just something about leaving a Super Bowl party early to catch Downton Abbey or another favorite on Masterpiece Theater that I've always savored. It's a secret haven of mine, my thrift store armchair in the basement where I throw an afghan over my lap, pull up the side table holding my hot tea with milk and one modest spoon of sugar, and lose myself in another world. The period dresses of Jane Austen's heroines, or the footage of the Duke of Cambridge and his family on tour, or the nostalgia and respect in each episode of The Crown – I'm captivated by all of it. As I dip my McVitties Chocolate Digestives in my tea, I escape to a place where tradition is honored and modern-day life is still steeped in civility. I am only slightly embarrassed to **admit that** I ordered a replica of Kate's wedding ring (previously Princess Diana's) on Amazon, or that I dressed up as the Duchess of Cambridge for Halloween…twice. I have a pop-up card of the full royal family (Charlotte and Camilla included!) that I keep on my desk, right next to my cup warmer and my solar-powered Queen Elizabeth who waves to me as her miniature Pembroke Welsh Corgis wag their tails. Friends have teased me, calling me Grandma because of my old-fashioned preferences, but I'll take it. I never met a grandma I didn't like – including Maggie Smith's Dowager. —

There are probably other people who would love to leave a crowded Super Bowl party early to catch Masterpiece…but there are also plenty who would hate it – which makes this student's "savoring" of it that much more unique and memorable.

The detail here is great, down to the fact that an afghan is a knitted blanket. This student knows this world and shares it with us in enough detail that we can visit it with her.

Good! She's not overly embarrassed because she owns it – she embraces this quirk of hers – and she's courageous enough to share it with us even if slightly embarrassed. She lets us see her as she actually is.

Both show us proof of her love of England in the action of dipping her specifically British cookies, and also tells us what she loves about these episodes and news pieces that she escapes into, which tells us more about what she values.

Great detail in this catalogue of evidence for her love of all things English.

Further proof of her self-confidence in owning who she is.

Clever, and a final example of how she knows this world inside and out.

V. WHAT SELECTION COMMITTEES ARE REALLY LOOKING FOR IN THE ACTIVITY SECTIONS OF MOST APPLICATIONS

1. DISSECT THE INSTRUCTIONS

The worst thing you can do on any college or scholarship application is to fail to follow the application's instructions. Aside from the institutional reasons for their existence, they also help to ensure that all applicants are judged equally. Ignoring instructions signals disregard for the process or an inability to pay attention, neither of which is good.

That said, the reasoning behind the instructions might not be clear.

Here we have annotated the "activity" instructions for the Common App — the part where you describe the activities in which you participate. This is the first section of the Common App that isn't straight fill-in-the-blank. Again, if institutions don't accept the Common App itself, chances are their instructions and questions are similar, and the strategies outlined in our annotations below will still apply. Most applications proceed in the same order, which is how our chapters are organized: from the basic demographic information to the Activities Section, to the Short-Answer and full Application Essay. We dissect the instructions for the Activities Section here and will likewise annotate the directions of various essay prompts in the chapter that addresses the essay sections.

We've chosen the Common App activity section instructions because they're likely to be directly applicable to you and are also typical of most applications, whether they are for colleges and universities that don't accept the Common App or for which you've chosen to use the institutional applications, or for any number of scholarship applications.

The text below is the actual language used on the Common App, and the notes to the side are our comments on those instructions. In addition to reading through them, you should make your own account on the Common App website to review the instructions and start interacting with the site as soon as you can in your own process. Navigating the site will increase your understanding and self-sufficiency, which will pay dividends throughout the application process.

The Common App – Dissected Instructions for the "Extracurricular Activities and Work Experience" Section

Reporting activities can help a college better understand your life outside of the classroom. Your activities may include arts, athletics, clubs, employment, personal commitments, and other pursuits. Do you have any activities that you wish to report? Y/N

Order of Activities:

- You may select up to 10 activities.
- Please list your principal activities in order of importance to you (you can change the order by using the up and down arrows on each activity).

Summer Job/Activity:

- Please list the summer job/activity with your rising grade. For example, if you have already completed the 9th grade, list your activity with the 10th grade.

1. Activity type:

2. Position/Leadership description and organization name, if applicable:

3. Please describe this activity, including what you accomplished and any recognition you received, etc.:

4. Participation grade levels:
   - ❏9
   - ❏10
   - ❏11
   - ❏12
   - ❏Post-graduate

5. Timing of participation:
   - ❏School
   - ❏Break
   - ❏Year

6. Hours spent per week:

7. Weeks spent per year:

8. I intend to participate in a similar activity in college:
   - ❏Yes
   - ❏No

2. GIVE YOURSELF CREDIT FOR GOING THE EXTRA MILE

You don't have to found an orphanage in Kenya to have a highly competitive application. But if you happen to have gone above and beyond in some way, then by all means include that when completing the activity section of the application – don't just list activity titles like a resume. You're given about 100 words to describe your contributions for a reason. Use that space to explain your impact as well as you possibly can.

First, think about the clubs and organizations that mean the most to you. Then consider any of the following as ways to highlight how your involvement made a difference to the organization and, if applicable, the wider community:

- Official leadership positions
- Areas of extensive planning and/or significant impact
- Instances where you identified problems and proposed solutions
- Additional efforts you put into the sustainability or success of the organization
- Occasions where you filled in for other people
- Times you were credited for acting "beyond your years"
  (taking on additional responsibility, such as replacing an adult or handling an emergency)

The following examples show you how others have quantified their involvement with varying degrees of success. For means of comparison, these five examples illustrate how people described their contributions to one of the most common student organizations, National Honor Society, or NHS. (For more examples of how to maximize the opportunities of the detailed activity sections, see section four of this chapter).

National Honor Society Example 1: Less Competitive

Activity	Year	Position	Hrs/wk	Wks/yr
National Honor Society	9 ❑			
	10 ❑			
	11 ☒	Participant	1	30
	12 ☒	Participant	1	30
Contributions, Leadership Positions Held, Activities:	I completed 40 volunteer hours with NHS.⌐			

At least this student has used the space provided to quantify her contribution in some way, but NHS is a service organization, so being a member and earning volunteer hours is a bit redundant. More compelling would be a story about her favorite volunteer activity that includes the number of hours.

National Honor Society Example 2: Less Competitive

Activity	Year	Position
National Honor Society	9 ☐	
	10 ☐	
	11 ☒	Member
	12 ☒	President

This is the most common reason an applicant has a less competitive detailed activity section: he or she leaves it blank. This is a missed opportunity to tell more of your story, and instead leads the reviewer to wonder if you just didn't know better, or whether you're disengaged by the activity, or by the institution or scholarship. Fill out the application completely by providing more details as requested (the available space isn't just an invitation for you to take or leave, it's a request for you to provide more information).

Contributions, Leadership Positions Held, Activities:

National Honor Society Example 3: Competitive

Activity	Year	Position	Hrs/wk	Wks/yr
National Honor Society	9 ☐			
	10 ☐			
	11 ☒	Member	1	30
	12 ☒	President	1.5	32

Indicates a specific leadership role

Contributions, Leadership Positions Held, Activities: I created a winter talent show that generated over $800 for the local animal shelter.

Quantifies the impact of her work

National Honor Society Example 4: Competitive

Activity	Year	Position	Hrs/wk	Wks/yr
National Honor Society	9 ☒	Member	1	30
	10 ☒	Member	1	30
	11 ☒	Secretary	2.0	30
	12 ☒	Vice President	2.0	32

This student has participated for four years in a row, with increasing levels of leadership, showing depth of involvement and length of commitment.

Contributions, Leadership Positions Held, Activities: As Volunteer Coordinator, I went around to local organizations to find places that needed volunteers and then matched students to projects at each of those organizations.

This indicates that the student has gone beyond the school walls and worked with local professionals, as well as made an impact on the club by both increasing possible placements and by matching students with those volunteer positions.

Still, there is no mention of the student's time as Secretary or Vice President, or of particular accomplishments or activities that distinguish this student or chapter from others. Strong…and there could be more detail provided.

National Honor Society Example 5: Highly Competitive

Activity	Year	Position	Hrs/wk	Wks/yr
National Honor Society	9 ☐			
	10 ☐			
	11 ☒	Treasurer	2	34
	12 ☒	President, Student Sponsor	4	36

While the student only participated for two years, we see formal leadership positions from the beginning (which is difficult in being a new member), as well as increasing levels of leadership from Treasurer to President to Student Sponsor

Two areas of specific service help us picture the impact of those 70 members, and indicate further leadership of the student since he had the role of coordinating them.

Shows that he stepped up when no one else did. He identified a problem and engaged in an act of leadership by taking on the additional work and responsibility of revitalizing the club while remaining factual and therefore not introducing arrogance into his response.

Contributions, Leadership Positions Held, Activities: When our faculty sponsor took a sabbatical this year, no one took her place and membership fell to eight students. I helped preserve 25 years of NHS tradition by becoming the "student sponsor," raising membership to seventy students, and coordinating tutoring programs and food drives.

This indicates impact, answering the question, "If not for this student, what may have happened?" Not only would the community have lost out on the services that NHS students provide and the students lost out on volunteer experience, but a school tradition would have died.

That's about nine times what it was when he started!

54

You don't have to be the president of an organization to have a highly competitive application. This student has been involved for four years at increasing levels of leadership, showing both length and depth of commitment

National Honor Society Example 6: Highly Competitive

Activity	Year	Position	Hrs/wk	Wks/yr
National Honor Society	9 ☒	Member	2	36
	10 ☒	Member	2	36
	11 ☒	Historian	3	36
	12 ☒	Secretary	3	36

This tells us the student goes beyond minimum participation and also details particular interests and academic strengths.

Contributions, Leadership Positions Held, Activities: Built rapport between school and community by founding and organizing open houses for community organizations to meet potential volunteers. Served as French, biology, chemistry, history, and writing tutor for walk-in program. Provided leadership through coordination of at least one class-sponsored event annually.

Another beautiful way of quantifying unofficial leadership positions.

This shows us that the student took initiative by identifying a problem (community organizations didn't know the volunteers) and creating a solution by assuming an unofficial leadership position (founder and organizer of open houses). This is sometimes more compelling than a formal leadership position, because the student is thinking and working in ambiguous situations to create a better outcome.

Other Highly Competitive Examples

As a point of comparison, here are a few more examples from actual applications that illustrate how students have effectively captured their impact in organizations other than National Honor Society. As you read the examples below, think about both how the students have gone above and beyond other participants in these activities and how they've explained their experiences so that you can understand their contributions.

Activity	Year	Position	Hrs/wk	Wks/yr
Black Student Alliance (BSA)	9 ☒	Member	1	36
	10 ☒	Member	2	36
	11 ☒	Vice President	3	36
	12 ☒	Vice President	4	36

This student has remained involved throughout high school, increasing the amount of time he's put in and serving as Vice President for two consecutive years, which speaks to his dedication and increasing responsibility in the organization.

Contributions, Leadership Positions Held, Activities: Certificate of Appreciation (9), Service Award for Commitment and Dedication (10). BSA is important to me because it provides all of the African Americans at my school, as well as people of different races who are interested, with an organization that promotes unity and learning about African American culture, tradition and heritage. It also gives me a way to serve my local community by reading to underserved elementary students, organizing an annual BSA church service for my school, and visiting the elderly at a local nursing home.

These means of recognition show that even before he took on a formal leadership position, this student was making a meaningful difference in this organization (leadership) and being recognized for his service, as well as his commitment and dedication (character).

Speaks to the student's values of honoring his culture and continuing to learn, as well as his openness to others who are different from him.

Broadens his circle of impact to extend beyond the school and gives us specific examples of acts of service that we can then picture him performing.

Activity	Year	Position	Hrs/wk	Wks/yr
Student Government	9 ☒	Class Representative	2	36
	10 ☒	Committee Chair (Homecoming)	4	36
	11 ☒	Treasurer	4	40
	12 ☒	President	12	52

In addition to the increasing responsibility inherent in this student's leadership positions, we see the increasing time investment, both in hours per week and weeks per year.

Ahh – this detail backs up why he was spending so many hours and weeks on Student Government in his senior year.

Contributions, Leadership Positions Held, Activities:

These specifics give us an idea of his informal leadership, as well as the impact of this school's particular Student Government.

With a new teacher who didn't have experience with Student Government, I was asked to organize the class and make sure everything was done properly and on time. I headed up the Staff Appreciation Breakfast, painting the student parking lot, homecoming and community service for the Senior Citizens Prom. I also inform the School Board monthly of what Student Government is doing.

This additional detail is important – not all Student Government presidents report to the School Board, and to regularly speak publicly to adult professionals is impressive.

Activity	Year	Position	Hrs/wk	Wks/yr
Einstein Bagels	9 ☒	Sales Representative	12	36
	10 ☒	Sales Representative	12	36
	11 ☒	Awarded Employee of the Month for outstanding commitment and leadership.	12	36
	12 ☐			

Great award to be proud of…and also happens to speak to common selection criteria

Contributions, Leadership Positions Held, Activities:

This unique detail, remembered years later, speaks to the student's powers of observation and appreciation of individuals. That bolsters her application, because it speaks to her character and service ethic, showing that she wasn't just going through the motions of her job, but was recognizing and connecting with the individuals she served.

I looked at work as a chance to connect with people. For example, freshman year I met this retired Navy Seal who ate at Einstein's every morning. His order was a blueberry bagel with one side butter, the other strawberry cream cheese. I saw him almost every day in the summer and on weekends during school. He would tell me stories from traveling, wars, cultures, foods, anything and everything from his life. When I stopped working there when I was 17, we began meeting every 2 months or so at the bagel shop to stay in touch and swap stories over bagels and coffee.

This speaks to the student's sense of commitment. As much as the number of years that she worked in her job, she clearly became dedicated to this one customer who turned into a friend.

This is an original take on personal contributions, highlighting how she sought to connect with others and – in the example she's chosen to share – how she honored an elder and a veteran by showing an interest in his experience.

3. LET'S PRETEND: SHIFT YOUR PERSPECTIVE

We won't know what you did unless you tell us.

Remember that activities and what they require vary from school to school. Depth of involvement and individual contributions vary from person to person. You know this. Just think of the person at the front of the room, leading the Student Council meeting – the one who's single-handedly building the class homecoming float on an 18-foot horse trailer, complete with an operable water feature. Then think of the kid asleep in the back. Both could put "Student Council" on an application, but they would mean very different things.

That's why it's critical to be specific and detailed in your application. Doing so ensures that reviewers will understand the full scope of your dedication and impact. So, pretend you're the reviewer, stick to the facts and share *all* of the facts. It's not bragging to accurately record your contributions. Let's walk through a few examples that show how generic activity descriptions can become more detailed and specific.

Example 1: Volunteer at Local Food Bank
  A. *Service Description, General:*
  - *Food Bank Volunteer*
  B. *Service Description, Detailed and Specific:*
  - *Volunteered 20 hours per week during junior year to collect canned food and coordinated food basket distribution with local food bank.*

From the first description, the selection committee can't tell what the student did. For one thing, there's no verb. Without a verb, there's no action, which means no specific person did anything. It also makes it possible for a reviewer to assume his minimal engagement—for example, that he sorted cans for two hours one Saturday near Thanksgiving.

The second example is much more helpful. Here, the student has quantified his contribution: 20 hours/week—basically a part-time job—for the entire junior year. Anyone reading his description will understand the depth of his involvement. It also makes it clear that he didn't just collect food but also coordinated its distribution, which demonstrates leadership. Lastly, reviewers know that he has gone beyond the high school to work with the local food bank and is making a contribution to the larger community.

Example 2: Religious Youth Group Member

    A. Service Description, General:

- *Youth Group*

    B. Service Description, Detailed and Specific:

- *Volunteered 10 hours/week during school to plan youth group meetings, lead discussions and select weekly readings. Raised $1,500 for annual five-day mission trip and served as crew chief, directing younger members in various service projects for over 40 hours each summer.*

Again, the more detailed description is much more useful to application readers. From this, reviewers know that this student didn't just show up at Youth Group meetings; she was a catalyst in organizing them. This student planned meetings, led discussions, selected readings and raised funds. By doing so, she shaped the organization and its members' experiences. The fact that she also served as crew chief for more than 40 hours each summer conveys her depth of participation and commitment to the organization.

Being specific and detailed guarantees you get the credit you deserve. Take a look at the examples in sections two and four of this chapter to see how being specific and detailed have helped previous applicants describe their activities and involvements in highly competitive ways.

4. HOW TO ELABORATE IN AN ADDITIONAL "DETAILED ACTIVITY SECTION" IF GIVEN THE CHANCE

Some applications give you the opportunity to provide additional information about the few activities on your long list that are most meaningful to you. This is a great opportunity to share more of what you value and what motivates you, so as to further distinguish you from other students.

To maximize this section of the application
- Complete it
- Provide information not already shared in the long list/resume page of the regular activity section (discussed in sections one and two of this chapter)
- Think about your detailed descriptions as short-answer responses (see Chapter VI) targeted to specific activities
- Speak to impact – both that you had on the organization and that it had on you
- Remember the selection criteria
- Be specific and detailed (see sections two and three of this chapter)

Some annotated examples of detailed activity sections that are less competitive, competitive and highly competitive can be found on the following pages.

Examples 1 - 3: Less Competitive

Name of Organization:	STEM Club
Years of Participation	9, 10, 11, 12
Hours/Week	8
Weeks/Year	40
Sponsor's Name	High School
Leadership Positions Held	Head of Scientific Process, Team Captain, President
Honors or Awards	Design award, master craft certificate
Personal Contributions	I came for the free pizza but now STEM Club is my favorite activity. Originally, when I wasn't leading, the team was poorly managed, and I couldn't live up to my potential! Once I took over and mentored the newbies, we cleaned our messy meeting room and made a game plan. Now, I'm club president, and our team has the skills to survive after I leave.

Nice leadership positions

Ick. See Chapter IV section six RE: how to share your accomplishments without sounding arrogant. There's no need to put down the leaders who came before him; the student could instead speak factually about specific challenges he and others on the team encountered and how he addressed them when he assumed a leadership position.

This is what we call an unintentional disclosure – even if this is true, it's not making the best impression to say that you joined a club for the food, rather than because you were interested in the activity.

What? Was a messy meeting room one of the most significant results of the aforementioned "poor management"? If so, the student's contributions (as well as the direness of the situation before his leadership) come off as that much more inflated.

Ouch. Aggressive and judgmental. Does not make readers want to meet this student or have him as a part of the school or scholarship community.

Again implies that if not for this student, the other poor saps in this program wouldn't have any hope. This shows no respect or collaboration, two characteristics highly sought after in college and scholarship students. It also gives no specifics as to which "skills" the student bolstered in his team. Providing concrete detail would make the response more factual and less arrogant.

Name of Organization:	Smart Kids Tutoring
Years of Participation	11, 12
Hours/Week	40
Weeks/Year	3
Sponsor's Name	Community Organization
Leadership Positions Held	Teaching Assistant
Honors or Awards	
Personal Contributions	I heard about a summer job online and contacted the supervisor to find out more, since I had participated in the program when I was younger. The supervisor hired me, and I lived at the campus with students at the camp, dealing with them during activities. It was definitely one of the best volunteer jobs of my life.

Nice – shows the student went outside of the school to contribute (which often requires more initiative than joining a school activity)

This chronology doesn't add much – it would be more helpful to hear about how the student benefited from the program and what led her to come back as an assistant. In other words, why was and is the organization important to her, and why was she motivated to volunteer?

Ouch! That comes off as judgmental. Better to say "helping them," "working with them" or "coaching them."

Really? Because there's no passion in this description. WHY was it one of the best? What was rewarding about it? Fun? Energizing? These activities should be ones that make you feel alive…and that make reviewers feel alive just by reading about your enthusiasm for them.

Name of Organization:	Allies (LGBTQ Club)
Years of Participation	9, 11, 12
Hours/Week	6
Weeks/Year	35
Sponsor's Name	High School
Leadership Positions Held	Founder (9), President (10, 11, 12)
Honors or Awards	I was awarded my school's Leaders who Make a Difference award for my work in starting Allies.
Personal Contributions	Club that stands against discrimination and harassment. Promotes unity and a safe space for students to come and talk about issues affecting them and their classmates to make our school a better place.

Again, a missed opportunity! This tells us what the organization does, not what this particular student did in this particular LGBTQ club – or what motivated her to do it. This would be a great place to elaborate on why she started the organization. What difference is the club making? Why does the student feel that's important? What are her priorities, points of pride and frustrations or disappointments?

Nice official leadership positions that impact the entire school

Examples 3 - 5: Competitive

Name of Organization:	Service Trip
Years of Participation	11
Hours/Week	115
Weeks/Year	2
Sponsor's Name	Community Synagogue
Leadership Positions Held	Day Leader
Honors or Awards	
Personal Contributions	Organized a $5000 fundraiser at my synagogue for the trip to help support our sister city through infrastructure improvements and community service.

There's space here to say where the destination was (Ex: Service Trip to Chicago, Peru, etc). If it varied over the years, there's still space for more detail, such as "International Service Trips" or "Service Trip (To San Francisco, Mexico City and other cities)." This specificity would help us picture the student's participation, as well as what's involved in organizing and going on the trip.

This is a missed opportunity. You usually have around 250 words here, so use them! There's so much more that she could have talked about here: what was the fundraiser? How many people came/flyers were circulated/volunteers did she supervise? What does it mean to be Day Leader?

This is helpful…and still pretty vague. What kind of infrastructure improvements and community service? What was she doing on a daily basis? What most surprised her about the fundraiser or the trip? What is she most proud of? Why is this one of her most meaningful activities? You get our drift…

Name of Organization:	Public High School Translation Services
Years of Participation	10, 11
Hours/Week	5
Weeks/Year	20
Sponsor's Name	Supervising Teacher
Leadership Positions Held	Only student chosen and allowed to assist
Honors or Awards	
Personal Contributions	Translation services in English and Spanish, leading class discussion, assisting both teenage and adult students in learning the English language. Was asked to continue work with the teacher in charge, Mr. Castillo, afterwards and kept in touch with a few students.

Great – speaks both to the student's skill and responsibility.

Speaks to the facilitation and public speaking ability of the student, in addition to his service ethic and language skill.

Illustrates the responsibility needed for these practical language classes, as well as the student's comfort with both peers and elders.

This is an indication of the student's good work and his teacher's positive appraisal.

This whole description is strong…and leaves us wanting more. What pulled the student toward translation services? What does he find fulfilling about it? What is important about the work, in his opinion? He could also share a short story about a student, Mr. Castillo or something that happened in class that was particularly meaningful to him in order to bring the example even more to life.

Name of Organization:	Soccer
Years of Participation	9, 10, 11, 12
Hours/Week	9
Weeks/Year	24
Sponsor's Name	High School
Leadership Positions Held	Team captain grades 11 &12. Starting varsity goalie grades 10-12.
Honors or Awards	1st team All-Conference goalie as a sophomore and junior.
Personal Contributions	I have played in two state semi-finalist games and led the team to three league championships

Great…and…? HOW did this student "lead" the others to victory? What were the particular challenges and strengths of this team, in these seasons and of this student as captain? Assumedly, there was at least one other captain, at least when the student was a junior. What was it like to co-lead? How did they work out their leadership dynamic? If none of that, what did it feel like when that championship goal was made? Why does she devote so much time to soccer? What does she love about it? This is a chance to make your application come alive!

Nice leadership positions

Great to include

Examples 6 - 8: Highly Competitive

Name of Organization:	Sonic Drive-In, Carhop
Years of Participation	10, 11, 12
Hours/Week	40
Weeks/Year	52
Sponsor's Name	Manager
Leadership Positions Held	I had to learn to become efficient at every job position in the store, including managing people.
Honors or Awards	I have earned a score of 100% on every mystery shopper who has rated my performance at my job.
Personal Contributions	I feel that I am a valuable member of the Sonic Team. I have routinely taken on the responsibility of other crew members when they were sick, came to work late, or just didn't put forth the necessary effort for completing the job correctly. I am a very proactive employee. When the store is slow and there is not enough business, I am one of the first people to begin doing other tasks, just because they need to be done. Being a self-starter and critically thinking problem-solver has greatly influenced my performance in this job because I am able to see a problem, know it needs to be fixed and figure out the appropriate course of action to fix the issue without taking others away from their work. I am proud of myself for being able to work diligently at Sonic and still maintain my grades at school.

40 hours/week year-round is a significant investment of time. Not only does this tell us that the student can hold down a full-time job while also carrying a full course load at school, but also puts the number of school activities and the leadership positions in those activities in perspective. There are only so many hours in the day, and if a student is spending 40 hours a week at work, in addition to 40 hours at school, there just aren't going to be that many to spend elsewhere, and we get that.

As we've mentioned before, both length and depth of commitment is compelling. This student has been involved for 3 years at increasing levels of leadership.

Indication of leadership role and skills, as well as trustworthiness and reliability.

These reviews provide an objective third-party assessment of her skills and back-up what she's sharing.

This shows us the student is dependable and a hard-worker without her having to brag on herself. She has told us the behaviors she engages in (stepping up, filling in) and has indirectly indicated that she IS the kind of person who puts in the necessary effort – because if she weren't, she wouldn't notice when that effort was lacking and her supervisor wouldn't count on her to fill in.

Don't hesitate to make claims about yourself! Self-starter is another way of saying "takes initiative," which is one of our observations from earlier sentences, but the need to think critically as she's taking on additional responsibilities may not have occurred to someone reading the application. Then, perhaps most importantly, the student backs up her claim of being a self-starter and critical thinker by breaking down the particular stages of independent problem solving that she uses at her job.

These provide specific examples of how the student routinely takes initiative, looks for things that need to be done and takes care of them – all examples of leadership. It also speaks to her character, as she doesn't just relax when things are slow. Instead, she has such a work ethic that she feels compelled to make sure she's earning her pay by filling her time doing work that will benefit her employer.

Name of Organization:	Track & Field, Cross Country
Years of Participation	10, 11, 12
Hours/Week	12
Weeks/Year	28
Sponsor's Name	High School
Leadership Positions Held	Awarded the Coach's "Hustle & Heart Award" for outstanding commitment and leadership.
Honors or Awards	Top varsity xc runner. Four varsity letters. Academic All-State 1st team. Winning Team in local Invitational. Marathon finisher. Race volunteer.
Personal Contributions	In addition to staying fit and balancing a busy life, running offers a cathartic and rewarding experience for those who embrace the running lifestyle. Running motivates me to reach my fullest potential by showing me how to dig deep and push my boundaries. I try to share my experience with running with others by leading the track and cross country teams in warm-ups, workouts, and races. I endorse self-motivation in high school runners and encourage my peers to run for themselves. I intend to keep running in college in citizens' races and running clubs. Depending on my performance in this track season, I am considering running varsity mid-distance track in college. Best finishes: 6th in the regional 800m with a time of 2:14:10 and 11th in our local Invitational (a mountain cross country course). Personal record in the 5k is 18:41:29 (6:01 mile splits).

Great award to be proud of…and also happens to speak to common selection criteria

This is a lot and speaks to the student's depth of participation.

Cool – we can glean from this that the student finds running to be cathartic and rewarding…even better if he were more personal about it, like in the second sentence. (EX: In addition to staying fit and balancing a busy life, I love running because I find it cathartic and rewarding.)

Details as to how this student has engaged in acts of service and leadership, be they with a formal position or not.

Quantifies the student's achievements

Continuation in college shows depth of appreciation for and commitment to the sport.

We're not sure what this means…could be more directly stated.

This is more specific than many responses that would stop with "to reach my fullest potential," which is somewhat vague and general, almost a cliché. Adding "dig deep and push my boundaries" tells us much more about this particular student's approach to and appreciation of running.

Name of Organization:	Museum of Nature and Science
Years of Participation	9, 10, 11, 12
Hours/Week	16
Weeks/Year	36
Sponsor's Name	Community Organization
Leadership Positions Held	As a Galaxy Guide and lead volunteer, I educate people about our universe, train new volunteers and help maintain and update exhibits.
Honors or Awards	I earned the Most Valuable Volunteer award my junior year and was the only student selected to direct daily shifts.
Personal Contributions	Supplementing my homeschool curriculum by volunteering at the Museum of Nature and Science is one of the best experiences I've had in my whole life. It allows me to meet incredible people: I've volunteered with a pilot, a Cambridge professor and a professional billiards player. I also have the chance to learn new things (like how to digitally stretch panoramic photos to create planetarium programs for projection onto the dome and how to archive images for museum collections so they'll be both preserved and accessible for years to come. And all this while educating people about a topic I know well and love deeply.

This number would seem high, but is supported in the description below and in the letter of recommendation from this student's supervisor. This tells us that she has taken advantage of the flexibility of the homeschool schedule both to pursue her academic passion and to give back through significant volunteering.

Illustrates length of commitment and depth of involvement

This is helpful for us to know, and humbly presented.

Ahh! So that's how she can volunteer so extensively.

This is helpful for us to know, and humbly presented.

Illustrates accomplishment while remaining down-to-earth by highlighting excitement.

There is energy in this writing, as she conveys specific details, showing knowledge and experience while also demonstrating enthusiasm.

VI. WHAT SELECTION COMMITTEES ARE REALLY LOOKING FOR IN THE SHORT-ANSWER QUESTION SECTIONS OF MOST APPLICATIONS

1. MINI ESSAYS : HOW ARE THE SHORT-ANSWER QUESTIONS DIFFERENT THAN THE APPLICATION ESSAYS?

In many ways, application reviewers are looking for the same things in both the short answer question and personal essay sections of your application. As a result, one of the best ways to improve your short-answer question responses is to look at them as mini essays. (So make sure to read the next chapter on essays and apply those techniques to your short-answer responses, too).

At the same time, there are some key differences between the application essay and the short-answer questions. The short-answer prompts are more focused than essay prompts and are typically directly tailored to the institution's selection criteria.

Trimming Short Answer Essays

Part of the challenge in these hyper-focused responses is in the name: short answer. It can be hard enough to prune your application essay to fit the 500- to 650-word limit, but short-answer questions generally ask for about 200-300 words. Thankfully, the prompts themselves are more direct, which helps focus your response. Still, the need to tighten your writing is more pressing than ever. We'll illustrate some specific techniques in the context of actual first-draft responses, but here's an overall strategy that works that we got from a former New Yorker columnist: read every sentence and shorten it by one word. That may mean simply taking a word out. But it may mean replacing two imprecise words with one precise one. Go through every sentence of your essay and shorten each by one word. Then do it again. Not only will you hit the word-length requirement, you will end up with stronger, more precise writing. (Again, the examples below are students' first drafts. We suggest areas to cut that will result in the end product being within the word limit).

Example 1: Select your favorite service activity, and describe why it is important to you and your community.

This is fine to leave, but if bumping up against your word count, this repetition is something you could do without. (Cutting both would save the student an additional 6 words, which could be the last 6 she needs to fit the requirement).

Student's first draft: *Music interrupts my dream… "Because I'm happy…" I slowly roll towards my alarm clock, whose cold, digital display reads 6:30 a.m. The sun is just starting to rise, and I think about lying my head back down on the pillow… "Because I'm happy…" I think there are a million things I could be doing on a Saturday morning. Sleeping, for instance. Or going on a run, visiting my sister in college, or*

66

eating smiley-faced pancakes. However, Pharell Williams completes my next thought: "Come along if you feel like that's what you want to do." Despite my momentary complaints, I decide that it's more than what I want to do—there's nothing I'd rather be doing every Saturday morning than getting up to work at Special Olympics with my favorite student, Jeremy.

Autism is a mental condition, present from early childhood, characterized by difficulty in communicating and forming relationships with other people and in using language and abstract concepts. A child with autism may have difficulty with communication, difficulty with social interactions, obsessive interests, and repetitive behaviors. Jeremy is an eight-year-old with a autism that causes him to have delayed motor and behavioral skills. However, through participating in Special Olympics, and being tutored each Saturday, he has consistently surprised me. Jeremy is not just my favorite person to work with because he's hilarious; he truly needs help, and it is incredible to watch him establish a connections. The sports and reading tutoring also have had amazing consequences for Jeremy's condition.

Since I began working with Jeremy on Saturdays last year, his fine motor skills, concentration and core strength have greatly improved, as well as his grades in school. Whereas before he was reading two grade levels behind, Jeremy is now on grade level and even asks his mom to take him to the library each week so he can check out new chapter books. What impacts me most, however, is the increase in his self-confidence. At the beginning of the year, Jeremy would barely touch other people or a book. Now, he feels secure enough to run short distances on his own and to read stories to his younger siblings. With this confidence, Jeremy is on track to excel in school and reach his full potential as a productive member of the community, despite his challenges. I cannot imagine another person or service activity that would make me so happy to get out of bed on Saturday mornings.

Although this sequence conveys humor and personality, it is unnecessary in a short-answer response and takes up space (36 words, in fact).

This whole section could be replaced with "...but" in order to save space and get more quickly to the point of the response: why she is getting up.

While the first two sentences of the paragraph explain the disorder & show academic ability, they distract from the focus of the response and use up 45 words. The brief description in the next sentence tells us all we need to know in terms of the purpose of this short-answer response: speaking to service.

THIS is the crux of the response: changes in Jeremy due to the student's efforts and, by implication, how/ why those changes are motivating to her, making this work rewarding and enjoyable for her.

This type of summary sentence is a good one to cut in short-answer responses, as the list that follows can stand alone while providing more interesting details. (Savings: 14 words).

Excelling in school is an example of reaching his full potential and it's difficult to predict too far into the future, so the second part of the sentence can be removed, saving her another 12 words. If she really wants to highlight long-term impact and has space, she could simply add "...excel in school despite his challenges, which increases his opportunities."

Ok...and yet ultimately, this student could have given more explanation about why this activity is important to her and to her community. Making the above cuts – and perhaps cutting this concluding line that doesn't add much – could give her space to add a sentence more about the organization's broader impact (such as "Jeremy is just one of the 1,000 individuals served each year. I'm proud to be a part of that effort because...")

Example 2: Describe a specific situation or activity in which you made a difference in the lives of others through your effectiveness as a leader.

Student's first draft: *As Student Body President, it was my responsibility to organize thirty students into committees so we could successfully execute our school's 50th Annual Homecoming. This event consisted of a school pep rally, girls' flag football, a softball tournament, a community parade and a homecoming dance. Each activity needed to attract the participation of a large and diverse array of students, both participants and spectators, as well as welcome community members. I delegated tasks and assignments to student council members to head these activities as well as to acquire sponsors from the local business community. Throughout the process, however, I remained available as a resource and gave students support and encouragement. For example, when one student had a misunderstanding with the softball field about the donated rental fees for the softball tournament, I spoke with the city manager and was able to not only receive free rental fees for the tournament, but a free year of golf at a nearby course as a prize for the tournament winner.*

One of the most challenging tasks was garnering the participation of other high schools in the county for the parade. Putting intense school rivalries aside, I put myself in contact with the student body presidents and principals from other schools and convinced them to invest funds into building parade floats and paying for the permit. This was an essential piece of the festivities because not only were we celebrating a milestone for our school, but the city as well. Our city was settled in 1840, and we were celebrating the 160th anniversary of the town's founding along the banks of the Animas River, and the town's historical legacy as the seat of our county. Part of my responsibilities included hiring pioneer actors and arranging to borrow livestock and a covered wagon for the parade. I also oversaw the parade safety and permit procedures by meeting with the chief of police, Martin Grady.

80% (and he should use the numeral) is more concise and entirely appropriate in the format of a short-answer response.

At the end of Homecoming week, I was exhausted but could declare that the programs had been a success. Between all of the activities, more than eighty *percent* of students and over *two thousand* community members participated. My work as a leader of *thirty students* translated into an enjoyable experience and a memorable celebration for the community.

2,000

Don't need to repeat this since it starts out the response.

Example 3: Pick one thing you really enjoy and tell us why you love it.

Student's first draft: *A lanky, blonde ten-year-old, scalpel in hand, voluntarily dissects a stillborn calf. This scene, taken from my childhood on a ranch, is just one example of one of my greatest interests in life: "playing" veterinarian. Since my grade school days, I have consistently felt the calling to act like a veterinarian. I am fascinated by the mysteries of animal anatomy, and through the act of dissection, I feel that the miraculous building blocks of life are being revealed to me. However, examination fulfills only part of my role as the "family veterinarian;" the job also implies that I care for all living creatures and their injuries.*

Reiterates what is stated in the preceding sentence, so this can be cut. (Savings=16 words).

Growing up in an isolated town on the Eastern Plains has given me the unique chance to be in close contact with animals throughout my life, as well as people who cannot afford basic health care for their animals or themselves. The occasional death of a pig or a stillborn calf has given me the chance to pursue my interests in dissection. For me, exploring animal anatomy hands-on is an experience both more reverent and educational than reading from a textbook. Inflating the lungs, examining the heart and its chambers and seeing how everything connects gives me a deeper sense of understanding and a respect for the miracle of life. Life is so mysterious, so intricate, and so exact that my brain is often astounded by the precision with which the organ systems work together. Nonetheless, the fulfillment I get is not just from taking things apart, but also in making things whole again.

Shortening this part of the sentence to "to care for people and animals in need" would clarify its meaning and trim the word count by 17 words.

This sentence could be cut, but the detail also reveals the interest and wonder of the student. For the short answer, she will likely need to omit it, reducing her response by 54 words. That said, if she chose to use it as the long essay in an application for a community service scholarship, she'd have space for this additional detail.

Whenever a herding dog scrapes a paw jumping out of a truck, a neighbor's horse refuses to eat or a pig goes into labor, I am at the ready

Could shorten this by 61 words by substituting "Over the years as my ailing aunt needed someone to take care of her animals, drive her to treatments, and administer medicine — and various migrant workers in the area have needed first aid — I have expanded my medical efforts to care for both animals and people."

to bandage, comfort and problem-solve. My goal is that, if possible, the animals can go happily on their way, free of charge to the owners. Over the past two years as my aunt struggled to beat lung cancer, I realized that the best way to serve her was to expand my veterinary role into the role of a nurse. She needed someone to take care of her animals, drive her to treatments and administer medicine, and I completed those tasks with a giant dose of love. On many occasions, I have also delighted in bandaging up workers at our ranch who cut themselves while roping, or sprained an ankle in the field. Through serving people and animals, I have realized that I actually fulfill my own desire to care for others.

My ongoing role as veterinarian has not only defined my personal development, but has brought me a great sense of fulfillment. Whether I

Choose one or the other, and save 2 words.

am dissecting an animal or sewing up a cut on my little cousin, I truly enjoy these experiences and opportunities to care for others. Playing the veterinarian on the block is something I love, and I plan on studying

Clear from other comments, so can be cut.

veterinary medicine in order to make my childhood enjoyment extend into my future career.

2. SPEAK THEIR LANGUAGE: TAILOR YOUR EXPERIENCES TO DIFFERENT SELECTION CRITERIA

Whether you are applying to get into college or to earn a scholarship – and since application cycles overlap, you'll likely be applying for both at the same time – every application's instructions will tell you exactly what the selection criteria are. The key is adapting what you've done to meet those criteria. After years of working in admissions and scholarships, we can say that most selection criteria include one or more of the following: academic achievement, athletics, leadership, community service, participating in a certain activity or hobby, pursuing a particular major or character/resilience/grit.

These criteria are useful to know because they help you identify institutions that fit you best. They also keep you from wasting valuable time applying for scholarships for which you're not even eligible, and they help you have a better chance of winning the scholarships or admissions you do pursue.

Think of the criteria as your key to breaking the secret code. They give you insight into why the institution might be asking each particular question or requesting different information about your contributions. For example, it shouldn't be surprising to see a question about community service in an application for a scholarship that lists demonstrated service ethic amongst its selection criteria. Reviewers for this scholarship will likely be reading responses to that question – and others – looking for demonstrations of that ethic, be it a student's passion and motivation for service, the depth of the student's participation in organized service activities, or the overall and lasting impact of the student's involvement.

Note: Knowing what your preferred institutions are looking for can also help you tailor your activity descriptions on the Common App. While they're very small spaces (150 characters for details, honors won, and accomplishments, and then 50 for position/leadership description and organization name), you can choose any of the selection criteria mentioned here to highlight attributes of yourself that you feel will round out your application as a whole and best speak to the institutions to which you are applying.

Be careful here. Selection criteria provide you with a means of determining how to tell a particular story that was important in your life, not which story you should tell to try to impress the committee (be that in the activities section, short-answer or application essay). Committees will always be more engaged in a sincere story that you're really passionate about than something you've devised because you think it's what they want to hear. (Trust us. We hear plenty of those, and they fall flat.)

To better understand how you can tailor your authentic stories through the lenses of different selection criteria, take a look at the example below in which we've taken a sample activity and described it differently according to three different sets of selection criteria—two directly from the Boettcher Foundation Scholarship application, and one a typical phrasing of a direct question seeking to draw out demonstrations of outstanding character. Note: this may look familiar because we're using the same prompts as those featured in the section on short-answer questions and annotating the responses. The difference is that our comments in the margins here illustrate that how the applicant chooses to tell the story highlights different selection criteria. Each criterion emphasized (in this case, leadership, service or character) is based on the prompt.

The student in our example is an Eagle Scout who preserved a maple grove for his Eagle Scout project. The four basic facts of his experiences are that a) he participated in Boy Scouts of America, b) was named Eagle Scout for a maple grove preservation project, c) was elected Senior Patrol Leader at camp, and d) led a difficult hike.

Here's how this student used those facts to respond to the Boettcher Foundation Scholarship prompt, **"Describe a specific situation or activity in which you made a difference in the lives of others through your effectiveness as a leader."**

> *During my eight years in Scouts, I always had my sights set on the highest award available: the distinction of Eagle. Because of this, I started planning my project early and attained the designation of Eagle when I was just 16. My project was to help preserve a nearby maple grove, to create an educational website and curriculum to help people learn about this endangered plant species and to share these electronic resources with schools in my district. In order to accomplish this*

Younger than most: answers the question "compared to what?" You could add, "whereas most Scouts don't attain Eagle until they're 17 or 18" to be as specific as possible, but most reviewers will know this and phrases like "started planning…early" and "just 16" imply that it was earlier than most, so you can leave the added detail out if space is at a premium.

Three-tiered project (does something significant, creates means of sharing it and communicates that to others). Goes beyond scope of many typical projects.

Shows breadth of project and impact.

multi-faceted project, I solicited volunteers outside of my troop, worked with the Colorado Natural Heritage Program and school board, divided volunteers amongst various aspects of the project and met often with each team to oversee the project as a whole. *I feel like the project was successful because I paired volunteers with parts of the project – outdoor work, website and curriculum design or relationship building – that matched their individual skills and interests. As a result, it was much easier to keep them motivated and to encourage participation in brainstorming how to make the project better.* Finally, I identified a committee chair from each area to present with me to the school administrations. Our resources are now being used in all of our district middle schools.

Shows leadership, people skills and management ability.

Tailored his coordination of volunteers for ultimate success of the project by leveraging their skills and increasing volunteer satisfaction.

Indicates that he is willing to share the spotlight.

Here's how he used those same facts to respond to the Boettcher Foundation Scholarship prompt, **"Select your favorite service activity, and describe why it is important to you and your community."**

My favorite activity is serving as Senior Patrol Leader for my Boy Scouts troop, which allows me to influence my peers consistently in a number of small ways. For example, on the last day of camp this year, we were supposed to summit Mount Wilson, one of the toughest peaks in the region. Unfortunately, many of our scouts were inexperienced hikers and started to show signs of altitude sickness early on. One of the younger scouts, Liam, developed a crippling headache and before we gained 1,000 feet, he threw up. I gave him my water, as well as some Rolaids from my First Aid kit to help him acclimate, and hung back from the other senior scouts to keep a closer eye on him and to help take his mind off things as we hiked. **When it started to rain, I started to worry about lightning.** Then when Liam's feet started to slip on the wet rocks and I noticed other scouts struggling as well, I knew that no matter how much everyone wanted to summit, I had to make the call to turn back. While this may not have had as broad an impact as my Eagle Scout project, *it made a bigger difference in another person's life,* so it's meaningful to me. I know I've been in over my head before, and am glad to know I could use my position to help someone else out and to model compassion and safety for the rest of the troop.

Sets the stage: puts us in the scene so we see and hear things as they unfold.

Direct service: illustrates knowledge, application of that knowledge, and both compassion and respect for the individual being served.

Note: in this example, the student has chosen not to go into detail about the impact of his Eagle Scout project. He may have referenced it in the Activity Section, or this may be his sole mention of it (which could then intrigue an interview panelist and prompt a question about the project).

Speaks to his values.

Indicates the impact of his service (as well as his own humility).

Here's how he described his Boy Scouts experience to respond to the prompt,
"Tell us about an experience that was integral to your character development and how that helped shape you."

On the last day of camp, my Boy Scout troop was supposed to summit Mount Wilson, one of the most challenging peaks in the region. About halfway up, however, it became clear that the weather wasn't going to cooperate. As senior patrol leader, it fell to me to make the unpopular decision that we needed to turn around. I felt the pressure to push on and help everyone achieve their goals, but I also knew that other scouts were nervous and some had altitude sickness. In my previous summers at camp, I had experienced the group euphoria of successful hikes and knew if we summited we'd earn points toward the Supertroop designation that we all wanted to achieve by the end of the week. At the same time, I knew that mild signs of inclement weather could rapidly worsen at such high altitudes and that members of our troop were already struggling. **Ultimately,** I felt it was my responsibility to look out for those who couldn't – or felt uncomfortable – speaking up for themselves. **In doing so, I feel like I secured the safety of everyone in the troop.** Some of the guys made fun of me on the way down for being too cautious, but I told them it was "Better to be a live chicken than a dead duck" and outlined a plan to earn the remaining Supertroop points through other activities.

Demonstrates the student's nerve. As Dumbledore says to Neville at the end of Harry Potter and the Sorcerer's Stone, "It takes a great deal of bravery to stand up to your enemies, but a great deal more to stand up to your friends."

Paints the picture for us so we feel the rub: amazingness of success vs. risk on the horizon. By understanding both, we can appreciate the difficulty of his decision.

3. GEEK OUT: DEMONSTRATE EXCELLENT ACADEMIC ABILITY AND INTELLECTUAL CURIOSITY BEYOND YOUR GPA

Not all schools offer Advanced Placement, International Baccalaureate or honors classes, but when they do, it probably seems that just about everyone against whom you're competing takes them. Add in the different factors of weighted or unweighted grades, grade inflation, personality conflicts and individual philosophies on achievement, and it's easy to see why a 4.0 doesn't mean the same thing at every school. So how do you stand out from a crowd of high-achieving students when applying for colleges and scholarships?

One of the best ways to bolster your academic profile in any application is by highlighting your intellectual curiosity. Geek out! Embrace your thirst for knowledge and the adventure of experiencing new things. Do this by underscoring areas where you took extra initiative to learn more (and where your behavior demonstrated that curiosity). When and where did you take classes that you didn't have to? Why? Do you read a book a week? Participate in Civil War re-enactments in your free time? One of our scholars took an extra AP stats class online during her senior year through a different school because she has a deep and abiding passion for statistics. (Yes, there is such a thing.)

Personal exploration, as well as extracurricular activity and course selection, can all point to intellectual curiosity. See the excerpts below for examples of how this has been done well.

Geeked-Out Short Answer Responses

The following students chose something to write about that they honestly delight in when responding to the Boettcher Scholarship short-answer prompt "Pick one thing you really enjoy and tell us why you love it." (Note: we're pulling our samples from Boettcher here, because our application asks for this directly. You can – and should – geek out in response to any prompt, be they the ones used as examples in the previous section of this chapter or the ones featured on the Common App.)

A common—and critical—error with these opportunities to discuss something you love is to pick something you think the committee wants you to enjoy (like AP Biology or recycling) and to write about it in such a flat and lifeless way that it's clear you don't. Remember: if you're bored writing it, the review committee is going to be bored reading it.

Take a look at the examples below and our notes on them to see the advantage of choosing something you truly love, even if it seems dorky or insignificant.

Example 1:

What?! This is awesome—puts us right in the action and makes us wonder "What's a Chipping Sparrow? Why is it in this guy's hand?"

This line might seem overly academic or insincere in other applications, but this came from an aspiring college professor who spends 20 hours a week working with birds in some capacity or another. As one of our committee members wrote in her notes recommending this student, "Dude LOVES birds!" It's an authentic application that resonates because it has different parts that back each other up.

An adult Chipping Sparrow squirms in my grasp as I delicately disentangle it from the fine mist netting. In this moment, I share an intimate, if unusual, acquaintance with this animal. I imagine all the landscapes it experienced, the thousands of miles it will yet travel; I hold a denizen of Yukon Territory and Mexico's high plains. Such singular perspective on bird migration fuels my passion volunteering weekly for Rocky Mountain Bird Observatory's spring and autumn bird banding program.

We believe this because he shows us in the first paragraph how his thoughts move easily from the science of conservation to the imaginative flight of fancy that allows him to picture where the bird has been.

As a local non-profit conservation organization, RMBO catches songbirds in mist nets to gather information on their migratory trends and physiology. The field station is a unique asset to the community; each day we educate visitors and school groups about bird conservation and migration. As I show off our birds, I sometimes discern a new appreciation for the natural world in a child's wide eyes.

Through educating and engaging the public and using our increased knowledge to improve migratory bird conservation programs, RMBO protects our invaluable natural heritage. Avian migration connects the world's remote regions and people in a way unlike any other natural phenomenon, which is why I am so dedicated to my volunteer service for RMBO's bird banding program.

He has earned the right to tell us this because he's shown it through his passionate writing and the hours listed in the activity section of the application.

Example 2:

Great hook. "A million WHAT? You own EIGHT of something?"

More than a million exist; I own eight. No, I am not talking about collectible stamps. I am referring to the board games that I craft and manufacture on school subjects to make learning fun across the U.S. Board game development has become a channel to use my imagination and fulfill my desire to create something exciting. Creating a board game is more than just writing hundreds of lines of rules and guidelines. *Let me tell you, it comes with dozens of errors.* However, these are what make the process so enjoyable. I cannot describe the satisfaction of solving each of them and finally watching friends play and enjoy the game.

In addition, the ability to blend features like current events, design and strategy into my games energizes me to *think about new possibilities.* After long days of classes and homework, working on my latest board game becomes a rewarding release. Solving the game, ensuring there are no errors or dead-ends and making sure the game is *fun* is not only therapeutic but also brings out the elements of determination, perfection and creativity of my character. It amazes me to see my hobby helping students across the nation. A student in rural Colorado can play the same board game as a student in inner-city New York, and supplement their in-school learning.

Example 3:

Not many kids would devour the pages of a world atlas, let alone use one as a bathroom reader. What a shame! Ever since I received my first atlas—a wrinkled, yellow kindergarten relic—an intense love for studying maps, cultures and languages has burned inside of me. Geography is essential in my life; it is a tool that allows me to understand the environment and my cultural identity, and also be aware of the world and its problems.

Starting with the geography bee in fifth grade, I became determined to memorize as much of the world as possible. When I advanced to third, and then second place in the state geography bee, I began to realize the value of geographic knowledge beyond facts on a page. Geography is a living science, and its hold on me still exists. *Poring through the latest National Geographic provides me with accounts of Mexican immigrants like my great-grandparents, an understanding of Nigerian oil politics, and human atrocities in Congolese forests.* And though I am not an expert in any geographic field, I believe passionately that all people are obligated to learn geography not only to snuff out ignorance, but to improve the world.

4. EXPLAIN YOURSELF: DESCRIBE YOUR MOTIVATION, VALUES, PASSION AND SERVICE ETHIC

Why you've chosen to do what you do is every bit as important as what you've done. That's why selection processes ask you to discuss your motivations, values, passion and service ethic – because each gives us more insight into you as a person. As a result, this is a great place for you to stand out.

Here's what we mean:
- Motivation: What factors have driven you to pursue the activities that you have? What inspires you to participate at increasing levels of responsibility? What spurs you on to continued levels of achievement?
- Values: Why is this particular subject, club or organization important to you? To your community? The world? Why is it important that someone volunteer in this way or that this cause not be forgotten? How does participating in this activity reflect your most deeply held beliefs or how you were raised?
- Passion: What is it that leads you to like this activity—recognizing that not everyone does? What specifically feeds your enthusiasm/obsession? What makes things that others could hate deeply appeal to you?
- Service ethic: What principles guide you in your service to others? What led you to choose a particular area of service? What drove you to contribute in the particular ways that you have?

Take a look at the following examples that speak effectively to motivation, values, passion and service ethic.

Example 1: Describe a specific situation or activity in which you made a difference in the lives of others through your effectiveness as a leader.

These two sentences set the stage by defining the problem. As a result, the student's next line comes in the context of answering that question – which tells us why he took the actions he did.

Many of my high school classes require daily use of a computer, so students whose families don't own a computer are at a huge disadvantage. During my sophomore year, I learned that our community library was going to pull dozens of obsolete computers from workspaces to be ground and recycled. I secured 60 of these computers to clean, re-format and donate to elementary school students whose families couldn't afford a home computer. My hope was that the students could better complete current assignments and would become more accustomed to the technology, helping them to use it later on. Before touching the computers, I had to receive permission from the library's chief information officer and from the elementary school principal, and to check the legality of distributing computers and software as I planned. I collected the computers, received training from an IT worker, and organized, instructed and oversaw a team of student volunteers to complete the computer restoration. As a result of the project, my district now recycles a number of outdated computers in this same way. Seeing the impact on students and teachers is the most fulfilling part of this experience.

This detail speaks to the depth and breadth of the project, which details the student's commitment and service ethic.

Further speaks to motivation and values by sharing his personal drive to do something (as well as the general over-arching issue with which he opened). This is what we mean by being specific and detailed.

This underscores sustainability and impact.

Example 2: Select your favorite service activity, and describe why it is important to you and your community.

When people ask about House of Hope, it's hard for me to explain because most people don't believe that a hot meal is very meaningful. However, they have no idea how much something so small can mean when you feel desperate or feel that there are few people who care. My mother lived in a battered women's shelter while pregnant with me until I was about six months old. When I entered middle school, we started bringing dinner to our local shelter as a small way of helping and bringing some hope to the people staying there. Seeing the children's smiling faces when we would bring in giant platters of hot, homemade food and they suddenly realized that they weren't having delivery pizza for the fifth time that week was always emotional and rewarding because, at one point, that was us. I always felt an extreme connection to that service project that I can't quite explain. It meant so much to me to be able to give to those who have experiences similar to my family's. Even though all they ever said was "Thank you," you could hear the extreme gratitude in those women's voices. In a way, I felt like I was helping a past version of my mother and myself.

This straightforward sentence gives us insight into why the project resonates so much with the student, and sheds light on her values of reciprocity and giving back.

Tells us that this student does know how meaningful seemingly small acts of service can be, and that she wants to serve others because she understands and appreciates that impact.

This, coupled with the student's sharing her family's experience above, speaks to her motivation to pursue and maintain this service activity. It also provides insight into her values, passion and service ethic.

Example 3: Describe a specific situation or activity in which you made a difference in the lives of others through your effectiveness as a leader.

Three years ago I helped start a STEM team at my old middle school. During one of our after-school meetings I was helping a kid that, although brilliant, was becoming discouraged. He had written several programs for a video game which had minor glitches. He kept getting frustrated when they wouldn't work. After the meeting he seemed like he wanted to quit STEM team; it was just too stressful. I asked him what Edison had said after failing so many times at making the light bulb. He naturally knew the famous quote, but hadn't applied it to video game programming. The next day we talked through his program and played the video game. He fixed the errors and was able to use those programs successfully in competition. I was really proud of him, and he had a strong sense of accomplishment after that. The following summer I saw him at a swim meet and he was so excited for the next STEM season and had all sorts of great ideas for the video game. That's exactly how I felt, and I couldn't be happier that he was so excited too! That's the kind of thing that really makes me love mentoring STEM.

Speaking of the younger student compassionately like this reveals the applicant's care and connection

The applicant's phrasing here is completely empathetic: not "the student thought it was just too stressful," but "it was just too stressful." This empathy, along with the compassion above speaks both to his motivation and his values.

You can feel his genuine excitement in these lines. It's this passion that fuels his service.

VII. WHAT SELECTION COMMITTEES ARE REALLY LOOKING FOR IN THE APPLICATION ESSAY SECTIONS OF MOST APPLICATIONS

1. ULTIMATE COSMIC POWER: MAXIMIZE THE OPPORTUNITIES OFFERED BY THE APPLICATION ESSAY

Students consistently tell us that the personal essay is the single most paralyzing factor of the college or scholarship application. But it's also the one over which you have the most control and that offers the most opportunities for you to present yourself the way that you'd like to be perceived. So, start thinking of the essay not as a problem, but as an opportunity.

The essay is your chance to:

- Tell reviewers something that resonates with the rest of your application. If you've listed a number of ways that you are involved in the arts on the activities form while telling us in the detailed activities section and short-answer questions that you love to share your passions with children, then your essay will probably expand on this interest and service.

- Talk about something that makes you unique. The tricky part here is that we often don't see something that makes us unique as anything special. See Chapter IV, section four for more information on how to identify key pieces of your identity that are unique to you, but here are some quick suggestions: taking care of relatives, overcoming family hardships (more on this later), a hobby or interest that you're obsessed with, where you work and what that says about you. Your individual circumstances distinguish you from other applicants by nature of them being individually yours.

- Set the mood that you want to imprint on the reviewers' minds. When they think of you, you want the feeling that's called up in their memories to be the one you established in your essay.

- Demonstrate reflection, self-awareness and originality.

- Provide an explanation for an "off" semester in grades or participation if what caused this academic blip is the topic of the essay (you could also just reference it quickly in the special circumstances or additional information sections if you want to write your essay about another topic).

- Demonstrate why you are a good candidate for the school/scholarship.

- Showcase your ability to communicate clearly, succinctly and in a compelling way.

2. FOLLOW INSTRUCTIONS AND RESPOND FULLY TO ESSAY PROMPTS

If you want to know what admissions officers and review committees want in an essay, the answer is in the prompt. Knowing this will help you pick the prompt you can best respond to whenever you're given a choice (as you will be on the Common App) and help you craft your essay effectively. Below, we dissect the five essay prompts provided in the 2016-2017 Common App to give you insight into what committees will be looking for as they read your responses. Even if you don't plan to complete the Common App, many institutional applications use the same or very similar questions and prompts. With all of them, the secret is embedded in the prompt. (Note: if you'd like to see annotated samples of actual application essays, see the last two sections of this chapter.)

Dissected Instructions and Essay Prompts

What's shown in italics is the actual text from the essay instructions for the Common App, and what follows is our analysis of what that text means.

Instructions: The essay demonstrates your ability to write clearly and concisely on a selected topic and helps you distinguish yourself in your own voice. What do you want the readers of your application to know about you apart from courses, grades and test scores? Choose the option that best helps you answer that question and write an essay of no more than 650 words, using the prompt to inspire and structure your response. Remember: 650 words is your limit, not your goal. Use the full range if you need it, but don't feel obligated to do so. (The application won't accept a response shorter than 250 words.)

This introduction is telling you why there's an essay in the first place: the college wants to know you, not a list of test scores and accomplishments which reviewers will see in other sections of the application. The specific prompt you choose — if you get a choice, which is increasingly common — should be of real interest to you and help distinguish you from other candidates.

Don't write like an academic lecture. On the other hand, you'll want to be more formal than the way you talk to your three-year-old cousin over Thanksgiving turkey, or the way you talk when you text your friends. There's nothing inherently right or wrong about any of these ways of speaking, it's just that each is appropriate in one setting and out of place in another. You wouldn't speak Swahili in Moscow or Thai in Buenos Aires; likewise, you wouldn't put LMAO in a college essay. You can strike a natural yet mature tone if you picture yourself talking with a trusted, non-judgmental adult —say, an uncle or aunt, a teacher, a counselor, a mentor or a family friend.

Although 650 words is the limit for the Common App essay, 500 words is still considered an appropriate length. Anything less than that seems dismissive. Aim for 500 and use more words if you really have something to say. Don't fill out your space with fluff. And if you find yourself having a hard time fitting it all in, start with what's most important to you. Then see our tips for pruning responses in the section on short-answer questions.

Common App Prompt 1: Some students have a background, identity, interest, or talent that is so meaningful they believe their application would be incomplete without it. If this sounds like you, then please share your story.

The key concept in this prompt is an **essential and meaningful aspect of yourself.** Here you need to address:

- **What makes you you.** Your background may involve where you've lived, your cultural roots, or an adverse or unique situation. Your identity, interest or talent could be an event or a series of events which demonstrate your unique development as a person, or any particular interest or talent central to who you are that you haven't found adequate space to expand upon elsewhere in the application.
- **How this background, identity, interest or talent is so meaningful as to be critical to your application.** Don't forget this part. Many students get carried away with the story and don't get to why it's important. The story you tell must be central to the formation of your personality and therefore so meaningful that your application "would be incomplete without it."
- **So what?** How does your background, identity, interest or talent make you different from those who didn't have this experience?

Everyone has a story to tell. With this prompt, you have the opportunity to share something important about you that the rest of the application hasn't allowed you to share. The key is not whether you lived in a Tibetan monastery or won an Olympic Medal, but whether you can derive meaning from your background and circumstances. Do you take care of your younger sibling while your single parent works two jobs? What does that mean for you, for your sibling, for your relationship or for your outlook on life? Reviewers aren't looking for more achievements here, but for meaningful self-reflection.

Common App Prompt 2: The lessons we take from failure can be fundamental to later success. Recount an incident or time when you experienced failure. How did it affect you, and what did you learn from the experience?

The word "failure" on a college application may make you uncomfortable. However, this prompt offers a really cool opportunity. If you succeed in addressing the following three parts of the prompt, you will handle the challenge well and will certainly stand out from those who are trumpeting nothing but their own successes:

- **What happened?** Describe the situation with clear, factual language as objectively as you can. Don't pad your account with too many details, and don't angle for sympathy (you don't have to – you'll earn it honestly by recounting the facts).

- **How did you respond?** What were your emotions, thoughts and actions? Honesty is important—but be careful not to dwell on your lack of self-control or your more negative traits. It might be helpful to remember that how you were affected places you in a passive position (which is sometimes the case, of course). Making sure to address how you responded reveals your personality, character and values.

- **So what?** This is the crux of the essay. Your response should go deeper than a superficial lesson like "I learned to never wrestle with a polar bear again." It should demonstrate how you are different now because of the past event you described and what you have learned from your mistakes.

Common App Prompt 3: *Reflect on a time when you challenged a belief or idea. What prompted you to act? Would you make the same decision again?*

Again, in your response reviewers are looking for three parts:

- **What happened?** Who was involved and what was the belief or idea? Keep this short and direct.

- **Why did you act the way you did?** What compelled you to challenge the belief or idea? What is important to you about that issue and why?

- **So what?** How did your decision to act in this way change you? How will it shape your future actions or beliefs?

The idea or belief you challenged does not have to be someone else's; it could be your own. In explaining your response and reflecting on your course of action, one of your core values, such as a "drive for justice" should stand out. Choose an event that will reveal insights into your values and character, and tell that story.

Common App Prompt 4: _Describe a problem you've solved or a problem you'd like to solve. It can be an_ _intellectual challenge, a research query, an ethical dilemma – anything that is of personal importance, no_ _matter the scale. Explain its significance to you and what steps you took or could be taken to identify a solution._

This question is tricky because the description of a problem you have or would like to solve appears to be the most important part. It isn't. You are. The critical questions to answer are:

- **Why is this problem important to you personally?** What is it about that problem that interests you? Why do you think it's significant (even though others don't – or at least don't think it's as important as you do)? If you can set the scene, allowing the reader to picture the problem and its impact, all the better. But do it quickly; save most of your words for how the problem affects you and what you believe to be important about it. Describing this in detail will give your reader insight into what specifically matters to you…which could very well not matter to someone else. As a result, your response to the prompt will differentiate you from other applicants.

- **What steps did you take or do you think could be taken to identify a solution?** This speaks to your initiative if you have taken steps, and to your creative problem solving whether you've acted or just brainstormed possible types of future action. It also speaks to your resourcefulness and how you think. We're not looking for the "best" solutions here – we're not actually even looking for solutions. We're hoping to get to know you via the steps you think could get us closer to solving the problem. Which brings us to this last point:

- **So what? Why are these potential steps the ones you think we should take? What do they say about you as a person?** What does the fact that this problem and the potential steps you've outlined are important to you reveal about your personality? Everyone who responds to this prompt will be describing a problem, and many will choose the same one. Your job is to cast that problem in the light that you see it in, showing us why it's important to you and what that reveals about what you think is important in life. What do you value that this problem threatens? Some people may feel climate change is the most important problem we face. This could be because it threatens the extinction of the whole population (showing mass casualties to be a driving reason for the belief), or it could be because we're leaving a more serious problem for our children if we don't work to remedy it now (indicating responsibility and legacy are important to the person). Others may think an entirely different issue is more pressing for entirely different reasons. Knowing what is important to you and being able to communicate why, as well as the first things you think we should do about it, will tell reviewers a lot about what drives you and makes you unique.

Common App Prompt 5: Discuss an accomplishment or event, formal or informal, that marked your transition from childhood to adulthood within your culture, community, or family.

Colleges admit students for a lot of reasons: for their academic achievement, for their well-roundedness and service to the community, for their ability to articulate what is important to them—but also because they want those students around. A college that admits you is committing to having you be a part of its campus community for four years. You need to demonstrate that you'll be the kind of person who will fit in and be an asset. This prompt is a great way for admissions officers to judge your maturity and perspective as a potential member of their community. Your job in this prompt is not to oversimplify adulthood, but to focus on the transition. You can focus on a milestone event in your coming-of-age journey, but make sure you emphasize the personal growth process rather than a single accomplishment. Promising topics could include overcoming a challenge or disability, reaching a goal or recovering from trauma or loss. (NOTE: If discussing a challenge or disability, trauma or loss, don't be overly concerned that it will seem like you're playing for sympathy. It won't come off that way if you stick to the facts and tell the specifics of your situation directly. If something major has happened to you, it has undoubtedly shaped you as a person. Sharing it shows courage and reveals your character.)

- **What was the accomplishment or event?** Describe it emphasizing your personal reaction and experience. For accomplishments, what effort and time had you invested? What had you or others sacrificed? For events, how did you respond? What was the weight of the event's impact?
- **How did it mark your transition into adulthood?** How were you different after the event from how you were before?
- **So what?** How is this event or accomplishment meaningful within your specific culture, community or family?

Additional Advice Regarding The Common App (and others)

You may use the additional information area in the writing section to share relevant information about yourself that is not captured elsewhere in the application. This may be an appropriate place to explain gaps or weak points in your application, as well as extenuating circumstances that affected your academic achievement. The additional information section of the Common App allows up to 650 words with no minimum.

Not completing the additional information section of the Common App is a missed opportunity. Everyone has additional information that they can share about themselves whether it be something that speaks directly to selection criteria or merely more information about them as a person, be it interests, hobbies, etc.

That said, you should not feel obligated to complete the special circumstances section of other applications, as this more specifically relates to circumstances that may have impacted what appears elsewhere in the application. If you are facing a significant life event or come from a unique background or set of circumstances that are important to explain, either because they are central to your identity as an applicant or because they affected your grades, test scores, leadership or involvement, the special circumstances section is a good place to share that information with reviewers. If you're worried that you might be over-sharing, ask one of "your people" (See Chapter III, section three), key amongst them your counselor or college access advisor, to review what you've written, make sure that the circumstances are delivered in a straight-forward and factual way and double check that they are not overly elaborate or vague. [If it helps, a good example of something to include in the special circumstances section would be something like: "My mother is on disability and I work 40 hours a week to help support the family." An example of over-sharing could be: "I recently broke up with my boyfriend of three months. I thought he was a great guy, but he did X, Y and Z things (that are actually minor irritations)…"]

While the additional information section is located next to the essay prompts in the Common App, it could be located elsewhere and possibly called something different (and more specific, such as special circumstances) in institutional applications. If you'd like to use it to share more of your story, just know that most applications have a section like this and keep an eye out for it.

Before you submit your application, ask "your people" (See Chapter III, section three) to review your essay for clarity, mistakes and whether it fully addresses the prompt. Remember: don't give your reader any excuse to skim your application or get frustrated with you because you (and 99 other people) didn't edit effectively. And no, you can't just rely on spellcheck to catch these for you. It won't catch "To many crises were affecting my work," or "I volunteered by the see." In addition to misspellings, you need to be on the lookout for typos, punctuation errors, repetition (of words or meaning), dropped words, inconsistencies, unintended disclosures and unintended consequences. We still chuckle about the student body president who wrote that she was "in charge of student body functions." Using the synonym "events" would have served her better and avoided an unintentional reference to the gastrointestinal tract.

3. BEING AUTHENTIC IS MORE IMPORTANT THAN TRYING TO IMPRESS US

One of the downsides of reading applications is that people try to impress us.

We get it. There's a lot on the line. But think about that kid in your class who has a massive crush on someone—you know, the one who just happens to loiter at the corner of the hallway where he or she knows the crush will walk by after class, who stocks his or her locker with the crush's favorite books and who just happens to have all of the crush's favorite obscure artists on his or her Spotify. Trying too hard makes a person look bad.

Do Your Best, Authentic Work

So rather than picking all of your essay and short-answer response topics by way of what you think we want you to be interested in (world peace, climate change, the economic stability of colonial America…), please, please choose things you are actually interested in.

Here's why:
- We read a ton of essays about the same topics that students think are the "right" ones. If you choose something you're passionate about, it will be a welcome change of pace.
- When you try to pretend to care about something, you invariably write about it in a way that proves you're just pretending to care. And if you don't care, why should we?
- If you write about something that energizes you, that energy translates into your writing and jumps off the page into our hearts and minds. That's the kind of reading experience that we want. That's what lets us get to know you as a person.

Authentic writing that demonstrates the courage to share your true self is more impressive than any false impression you could construct. It's also refreshing to someone who spends countless hours reading essays about things someone thinks they want to hear about in a generic pseudo-academic voice. And something that is refreshing is also memorable.

Even so, this is easier said than done—especially when it's a piece of writing that will be read by strangers. Here are some key strategies to help you out:
- Don't try to be funny if you're not funny, or philosophical if you're not philosophical. Be what you are. That's infinitely more interesting than any front you could put on.
- Remember that things that just seem normal to you can be really interesting to others.

Not everyone comes from where you do, or has such intimate knowledge of shark fishing, improvisational theater or World of Warcraft. If you explain your true passions in detail, we'll be hooked.

- If you're absorbed in the topic, we will be too.
- Give us a picture of who you are and an understanding of your character and personality, and your essay will stand out. We will have read countless indistinguishable essays by that point, but yours will be the first that captures your personality.

Write the Way You Speak (To the Boss)

Whatever your personality or topic, your essay should be written in your natural voice. "Hearing" you through your writing is one of the ways we get to know you through your application. Here are two examples of students who have done this well.

Example 1: Evaluate a significant experience or achievement that has a special meaning to you.

Casual, personal intro tells us this student is about to tell us a personal story.

Looking back, I probably should have been more panicked. Most people would scream, or call out for help. I just lay there, desperately trying to wiggle my toes. The cool grip of the mat brought me back to reality, and as I opened my eyes through the blur of tears to the horrified heads bobbing around in my peripherals, I knew the fall had been spectacular.

Words like "panicked," "wiggle," and "spectacular" give this essay the rings of truth—we believe this student is telling us a legitimate, personal story.

Some students might avoid a loaded word like "stupid" for understandable reasons. This student uses it effectively by giving examples of the questions, then following them up with his inability to answer, demonstrating that "stupid" is his point of view at that moment in time.

As I lay there, a paramedic materialized and began asking me stupid questions, "You see the Rockies game last night? Ever been to Cincinnati?" As I attempted to answer, my words came out slurred and incoherent. How could this idiot be quizzing me about MLB trivia while the boulder seemed to be growing heavier by the second? I was numb as my tears fell onto the stretcher and we passed fish-eyed parents into the parking lot. It's important to note that I wasn't crying because of the pain. I was crying because those looks, the paramedics' attempt to distract me, meant something terribly real had happened, something impossible.

By this point, we realize that the phrasing of the question is meant to put us in the his mindset during the immediate aftermath of his fall. We realize alongside the student why the medics are asking these questions. Thinking they're idiotic is a result of the shock and incomprehension of the moment.

Another unique, real choice of words that we can imagine the student saying to us.

Powerful, harsh, expression of his emotional state. Sharing what you hate can be just as effective as sharing what you love. The key here is that he isn't intolerant or aggressive. His honesty about his anger during that time – anger that he then channels into his recovery – shows real courage.

My next few weeks bled together with no end in sight as I wilted on our living room couch from dawn until dusk, staring blankly at whichever program my mother left on the TV. It seemed the only way to tell one moment from the next was by the never-ending lineup of Nike commercials. I hated them. I hated seeing the athletes doing what they loved, chanting their mantras: "Just do it. One more. Impossible is nothing." I found the superlative nature of the last quote especially aggravating. Impossible had to be something. For instance, trying to keep it together when the doctor explains the slim chance of a return to the sport which you love, that was quite impossible and it sure as hell wasn't nothing.

This is the core of the essay. While some may have omitted the depressed and bitter feelings, this student takes us into the heart of them and that rawness, that anger, is so relatable that it draws readers in. His vulnerability makes us trust him, care about him and remember him even more.

…And we begin our upward climb…

You can imagine my excitement when the doctors finally signed off for a first practice. It didn't matter every skill now came with a perpetual question mark: is this where it happens again? I could at least be myself again, if only for one hour every other day. Those one hour practices turned to two hour trainings, and in nine months I'm more confidently myself than I ever was before, with the 2016 Olympic Trials firmly in sight and a new catchphrase to lead the way: Impossible is nothing. Furthermore, impossible is a concept most people never fully understand, one I didn't come to grasp until after a tumultuous Saturday in January.

Doesn't leave out his continued doubts.

And there it is! He can be honest and bitter above because he has emerged on top of the ashes with a new attitude to match his renewed athleticism. Even without physical recovery, an essay like this could channel the disappointment and frustration into another activity or perspective to keep guard against bitterness.

Impossible means lying to the paramedics when asked, "Can you feel this?" Impossible means overhearing the doctor whisper, "We don't know what will happen." Impossible means losing the very drive and passion which once defined you. Impossible means returning to a sport your parents beg for you to quit because they're just as scared as you are. I've done all that, and impossible is nothing.

Beautiful conclusion that demonstrates his transformational journey.

Example 2: Discuss some issue of personal, local or national concern and its importance to you.

Nearly four million children in the United States under the age of 18 are diagnosed with food allergies. At the age of 18 months, I was diagnosed with severe, life-threatening food allergies to peanuts, tree nuts, sesame and shellfish. If I come into contact with or eat any of these

Many essays that answer this prompt start with a statistic like this. Few follow up with a weighty sentence that clearly states why this issue is of personal significance to the author.

foods, I will experience a severe allergic reaction, known as anaphylactic shock. When I was 10 years old, I experienced anaphylaxis on a camping trip to freshwater fish, thus adding another food to my list. Despite this, I do not let food allergies define my life. They may affect every area of life, but school and social life are the two most prevalent.

When I first entered preschool, there were no guidelines for or awareness of food allergies. When my Mom told a teacher I had food allergies, he responded with, "What's that?" Fifteen years later, awareness has been significantly increased in my school district, in Colorado, and across the nation. In school, especially at the elementary level, food is everywhere. It is a danger to be in a classroom that is distributing nuts at a party. My Mom and I helped spearhead an effort in my school district to establish safety guidelines to help severely food allergic kids. After many years of success in our district, that effort eventually became a statewide movement and, in 2009, I testified in front of the State Senate and the House of Representatives in favor of Senate Bill 09-226, which requires all school districts in the state to have guidelines to manage food allergies in school. My testimony convinced a State Senator to reverse his position and vote yes on the bill, which successfully passed both houses and has been in effect for three years. However, school is only one part of my life.

Social life can be a far more tenuous and dangerous area. Whether it's participating in classroom activities or going to a movie with friends, food-allergic children may take risks just to fit in. Parents across the nation are concerned for their child's safety. In response to such concerns, I began to write a monthly column in a newsletter for AllergicChild. com. This started six years ago and has continued to the present. Because of this column, I've had the distinct opportunity to be a speaker at four national conferences on food allergies and to help other kids across the nation live a safe and successful life with severe food allergies.

Anaphylactic food allergies are a hidden disability. However, I don't consider myself disabled. This is extremely important to me because I've worked tirelessly to assure that others across the state and nation can feel safe in school and with their friends. Some people think not being able to eat PB & J sandwiches may have been a loss to my childhood, but I've learned it is the things we don't have, and may want, that teach us the most about how to live a happy and productive life.

Make Them Want to Meet You in Person

A primary benefit of sharing your genuine self in all your honest passions and quirkiness is that it makes reviewers want to meet you in person, something they can do only by interviewing you or admitting you to their institution.

Take a look at the quotes below to see how others have made reviewers want to meet them by revealing their true selves.

Example 1:

I love to sing in my car. I can't carry a tune to save my life, but there's just something about belting out your favorite song that puts you in a great mood. In my car, where no one can hear me, I'm basically right up there with Pavarotti. Everybody sounds better when no one is listening. (That's most likely going to be a scientifically proven fact pretty soon ... ok, maybe not.) Singing in my car may not make me a superstar, and I might look a little dorky driving down the road, but it's the best way to make me feel great, really brighten my day, and I absolutely love it.

Example 2:

With a pink towel tied securely around my neck and my underwear worn proudly atop my miniature head, I gracefully dashed across the kitchen. I sought a damsel in distress, a sinister villain, or even a lost cat, in order to prove my virtue to the audience of stuffed animals and toy soldiers that sat before me, anticipating my upcoming escapades.

It's true. I've always wanted to be a superhero. And who wouldn't?

Example 3:

I have the loudest and most inconsistent laugh you have ever heard, guaranteed. One moment, I have a cute girly laugh and the next — I have an Eddie Murphy over-the-top laugh, by no choice of mine. My freak show of a laugh does not bother me, however, because I LOVE to laugh.

Example 4:

I'm embarrassed, but only slightly, to admit I get chills every time I hear our fight song. I have adopted our principal's deep pride and enthusiasm for our school, and these feelings have made my high school years more meaningful – and a whole lot more fun.

4. HOW TO TELL THE GOOD FROM THE BAD

We have marked the relative strengths and weaknesses of actual essays to be explicitly clear about how we draw distinctions between essays of different quality.

Less Competitive Essays

The following three essays missed the mark for the reasons indicated, and those reasons apply whether the essays were written for the Common App, a specific institution or scholarship, or both.

Example 1:

A Good Teacher

A person who has had a significant influence on me would have to be my Social Studies teacher Mrs. Espinosa. As a sophomore she taught me the basics of World History. She made this a very exciting yet informative class through all the projects and book work we did. Then As a junior, I enrolled in two different classes that she taught. The first one being Civics. Her knowledge and creativity again made this class very exciting. Then, I took Intro to American History. As a senior I am following that up with AP American History and the class is still very enjoyable. I would have to say that Mrs. Espinosa has influenced me in several ways. He has taught me how to work hard and not settle for anything less than my best. At the same time she has shown me that Social Studies can be very fun and exciting if you a willing to do the work. All of these things have definitely influenced what I want to do for a living, which will probably be in politics or government.

Annotations:
- *Random capitalization shows a lack of attention..*
- *Like what?*
- *How? Remember: the compelling story lies in the specificity and detail.*
- *Why/how? So far we have a list of courses (already detailed on the transcript) and some vague adjectives, but no specific images or anecdotes, or insight into what the student likes in particular.*
- *Unnecessary filler words, just like the opening sentence of this essay.*
- *She?*
- *Repetitive without additional detail or example. Also, "You ARE?" Again, these types of errors will catch the attention of review committees — and not in a good way. This also suggests there's more to the story that would also tell us something about the student. How/why did she realize that the subject took work and then was rewarding?*

We're sure you have identified many pitfalls this essay illustrates that you should avoid. For example:

- First and foremost, this essay gives us no insight into the student.
  - o We don't know how the teacher was knowledgeable, interesting and creative,
    OR what effect this had on the student.

95

- o It would be more helpful – and interesting – if the student wrote that she or he admired the teacher because she did in-depth research on original texts written on animal skins…or because she put herself through graduate school while raising her brother's children after the brother died in a car accident. Do you see how either – or any other specific example – would tell us more about the teacher and therefore the student?
- The essay is one long paragraph, which makes is a bit of work to get through.
- It "tells" us the teacher and courses were interesting, but never why or how. It would be more compelling if the student had told us a story of one particularly interesting or creative lesson the teacher had taught, allowing us to see both the teacher and student in action.
- The essay also wastes valuable space listing individual courses rather than focusing on the teacher and why the student chose to write about her.
- Finally, the essay, though short, has many grammatical errors that distract from what the student is trying to say and indicate either a lack of academic ability or a certain level of carelessness. If proofreading isn't your strong suit, find a friend, family member or teacher to look over your essay for you.

Example 2:

The title is not actually what this essay is about, as the student never mentions medical marijuana, but rather merely legalization and recreational use. ALSO NOTE: while all of the essay examples we're discussing here happen to have titles, this is not necessary, nor even a preference. If we had to guess we'd say about half do and half don't, and the choice doesn't matter. What counts is that the essay accomplishes its purpose, as our annotations point out.

The Unchecked Expansion of Medical Marijuana

We don't need to be told what the essay is about. Just jump into the topic to make the best use of your limited space and to capture the reader's attention.

This essay has to do with the issue of the spread of marijuana across the U.S. and its potential legalization. I believe that allowing marijuana to continue its spread throughout states such as Washington and Colorado would be harmful to the United States. By letting marijuana continue throughout the states, the government is saying that rules do not matter.

There's a fundamental flaw with this reasoning: If the rules are changed in a democratic way, the continued legalization of marijuana wouldn't be in opposition to "the rules."

If marijuana were to be legalized it would give a bad impression to the citizens of the United States. Many people would think that if you do not like or agree with a law, then all you have to do is break it and the law will be changed. Many people do not agree with marijuana being illegal and they continue to misuse the drug. By just letting people get away with it, the government is saying that people do not need to be punished for breaking laws.

Again, if it were legalized, they wouldn't be breaking the law.

This repeats the last sentence of the first paragraph. It would be more interesting – and tell us something about the student – if he told us why it's important to follow laws and have consequences if they're broken or what about the legalization of marijuana goes against his values. Why was this topic of such personal importance to him?

Since this is essentially an academic or position paper, it's worth mentioning that this claim is not supported by any data, which has the effect of it reading like hearsay.

It's interesting to note that none of the potential benefits presented by proponents have been acknowledged, much less refuted (even the one in the student's own title).

Another issue with the spreading and legalization of marijuana is that it would send the wrong message to the youth of the United States. The youth are the future of this country; their beliefs will become what this country is based on. I believe that this country has worked too hard to create a drug-free mentality in the youth to just give up. ———— —— Marijuana is seen as one of the safer illegal drugs out there. While many people start with marijuana, they rarely end with this drug. Marijuana is a gateway drug, allowing people to make contact with more deadly drugs. By making marijuana easier to access, you also make worse drugs easier to access.

By making marijuana legal, no problems would be solved. It would make it seem as though any laws could be changed if they are broken. There would be nothing positive for this country that would result in the legalization of marijuana.

It's nice to see what the student believes here, but we're not told why he believes it, nor are we really given details as to what he means in this statement. Why is legalizing marijuana "giving up" in the student's opinion? Why is a drug-free mentality worth cultivating and what would be the consequences of discontinuing its cultivation?

The primary detriment of this essay as an application essay is that it tells us very little about the student, since it appears to be an academic paper used as a substitute for writing an application essay (and it's a poor academic paper at that, because it is full of circular reasoning).

Remember: the purpose of the application essay is to give reviewers insight into who the student is as a person. It's possible for this to be done by taking on an issue of local or national significance, but only if the student shares his or her beliefs and values. An effective essay about an issue would clearly indicate why the student cares about the issue and was motivated to get involved with it – and to choose it as the topic of the essay.

More than whether the student is for or against a particular issue, reviewers want to know why. Filling the essay with his self would lead this student's essay to stand out regardless of how many other applicants chose the same issue. This student's essay, however, could easily be confused with anyone else's as the reasons cited are general, not personal or specific.

Example 3:

Shock

Opening is vague and a bit overblown.

Shock. When one's world suddenly crashes around him, the pain is not felt to avoid a complete obliteration. "You will not be able to play again." The words were potent despite the monotonous speech in which my doctor delivered them. Although my life has been riddled with various obstacles, the most life-changing one was the torn meniscus suffered in 2012.

Lacrosse has always been my love and now I would not be able to play for the rest of the season. I never saw the opponent coming, but they stole the ball and they stole my ability to play.

"The opponent" and "they" don't agree. Should be he or she.

You don't have enough space and reviewers don't have enough time to read empty sentences like this.

— Health is the single greatest opportunity that we have in our lives. It is also one of the most overlooked opportunities. Before this, I wouldn't have considered myself a person who takes his health for granted. In fact, ever since my dad was diagnosed (and survived) a rare form of cancer, I have thanked the Lord every day for my health and strength. This trait resulted in a bitterness inside of me. I couldn't figure out why something for which I was grateful could be stripped away from me. It was devastating.

The student tells us he had a bitterness but doesn't show us how he overcame it.

People say that struggle creates empathy. This is true for me. This event created in me an empathy for all people who have a health issue that has separated them from doing something that they love. None of us gets out of this life untouched, as I learned on that fateful day.

Again, this tells us something about the student rather than showing us the student in action and letting us decide he is empathetic.

What was that change? The essay doesn't show us the student before the accident, nor does it illustrate the hard-won transformation.

Tearing my meniscus is a significant personal experience due to the immense change that it inspired within me and my life. Today, the remembrance of that shock encourages me to pursue its opposite. I'm now much stronger for having lived to tell this tale.

How?

The melodramatic tone of this essay manages to reveal a lack of empathy while asserting the opposite. Comparing the student's inability to complete the lacrosse season to his father's rare cancer and others' injuries or disabilities that keep them from "doing something that they love" (much less from living autonomous lives or living to their full life expectancy) demonstrates immaturity and lack of awareness.

Students don't need to have experienced struggle beyond a torn meniscus (or losing the Student Council election or debate final), but their discussion of that struggle should illustrate a certain degree of understanding and perspective that is lacking in this piece.

Competitive Essays

The following two essays are solid examples of what we typically see in competitive applications. They, combined with the other application components, gave students a strong chance of securing college admission and scholarships.

Example 1:

The Culmination of a Dream

After a year of preparation, the moment of truth had come. I was at the Distributive Education Clubs of America (DECA) State Leadership Conference. The conference was coming to a close and the students who would become the new state officers for the upcoming school year were about to be named. These students would lead the 4,000+ members of DECA in our state into the future. I had invested countless hours of work in preparation of this moment. The process was by no means a popularity contest, but rather, a daunting two-day test in front of a panel of students and teachers where only the 12 best candidates would emerge as state officers. A speech in front of the entire panel and multiple interviews were just a part of this process.

I watched as a current state officer walked to the microphone. For a moment, the crowd became silent in anticipation of the results. At least, it became silent in my mind. The letter was slowly opened and after what seemed like an eternity, the names were read. I heard my name announced, indicating that I was elected as state president. I felt a great sense of accomplishment. What had begun as a dream, became a reality.

This experience was significant to me because I had failed to reach this goal the previous year. Prior to this year, I worked hard toward this goal, but had come up short. At first, it felt like all the speeches, all the interviews and all the hours spent creating flyers had been wasted.

But in reflection, I came to an understanding: what I lacked was experience. I realized that my time had not been wasted, but had established a great foundational experience. It gave me a year to mature and to perfect all the skills that I would need to become an effective state officer. It allowed me to hone my speaking ability and to perfect my interview strategies. It gave me experience. This maturation period allowed my leadership skills to flourish. I returned the next year extremely motivated and confident in pursuing my goal. The initial experience I had gained was a pivotal reason as to why I was elected the following year. I had to work hard and overcome failure in order to achieve my goal, creating in me a great respect for my position.

This experience allowed me to achieve a goal because it forced me to reevaluate how to approach success and failure. I am thankful for the experience I gained the previous year because I earned the experience of a lifetime the following year. The skills I acquired did not just make me a better candidate, but a better leader as well. I intend to use these skills as I lead the state DECA, as I progress into college, and in my future career.

What strikes us most about this essay is the honest discussion of failure, as well as the concrete examples of what the student proactively tackled in order to improve and to do better in seizing her chance at a second attempt. That she took that chance shows both courage and strength of character. Review committees are not expecting applicants to be fully-formed and have it all figured out, just to illustrate reflection and growth.

Attempting to overstate your development or presenting your current state as an end point could have negative consequences. We've read essays in which students have overconfidently stated their vast learning or asserted answers to complex social, economic or political problems and therefore inadvertently come across as naïve, immature, ill-informed or egotistical.

In contrast, this student shares one specific experience and her subsequent realization of the benefits of a setback that initially frustrated her. She could do better at tying the issue strongly to her particular ongoing path of personal development, which would give us both a clearer sense that she understands she's still learning and growing and also provide key insight into her individual values and motivations. In other words, why she, personally, wants to be a state DECA officer and how she's different than other students who want to be a state DECA officer. Yet still, this is a solidly competitive application essay.

Example 2:

A Man of Influence

At first glance, Malik Anderson is just another high school teacher. With his curly hair left natural, wearing a school T-shirt and jeans, he does not look like an extraordinary person, but he is the most amazing person I have ever met. Mr. Anderson is the director of my music department and over the past four years of my life he has helped me to find the person that I am today.

Mr. Anderson has a different approach to learning than most other teachers. He greatly believes that trial and error is the only way a student will ever learn how to succeed. Our music department is completely student-run, only advised by Mr. Anderson. This means that every student has the chance to work in a similar way to how professional companies have their technicians and musicians work. By allowing students to create for themselves, Mr. Anderson builds an environment for experimentation.

Without this environment I would not have discovered that I want to be a professional musician. Every time I had a question without a straight-forward answer, Mr. Anderson would make me figure it out, pointing me in the right direction, then letting me think about the possibilities. Mr. Anderson has kindled my creativity and allowed me to find my place in the world.

Many teachers do not spend more time with you than their families, but Mr. Anderson has managed to become a second father to those of us in the department. Due to the fact that we spend most of our evenings and weekends in rehearsal, he watched over us as if we were his own kids. One of the great lessons that Mr. Anderson taught me is to always respect the space you are working in and the people you are working with. Many people spend their time in the auditorium and if we do not respect it, it will be ruined and we will not be able to perform there anymore. Also if we do not respect those we work with, we will be stuck together for a year, and the process will be very painful. Mr. Anderson is always there if I need help and is always pushing me to do my best.

The first sentence highlighted here is a necessary explanation for those not familiar – and given quickly so that the focus of the essay remains on the teacher and student.

The 2nd sentence then tells us why the above is meaningful. Without this sentence (which most students would leave out), the essay becomes nothing but facts about the teacher and department.

This paragraph drills down deeper than the last, telling us how the above has impacted this student personally.

This sentence basically reiterates "second father," but because it's more specific than the first sentence, we'd recommend cutting "second father," which is a bit of a cliché.

This slips into generalizing a bit, but still provides some examples.

Four years might not seem like a long time to get to know someone, but in this time I have watched in awe as Mr. Anderson handled moody teenagers, cared for his aging parents and was diagnosed with multiple sclerosis (MS). I would not trade any of the time I have spent with Mr. Anderson. His perseverance and guidance have molded me into who I am. He inspires me to be the best I can be and I strive to be as influential as him one day. I will never forget what Mr. Anderson has done for me, and I hope one day to return the favor.

Not necessary — essay has already sufficiently ended, and how would the student really return the favor to Mr. Anderson, anyway?

Despite its shortcomings, this essay illustrates how to talk effectively about someone important to you while also revealing more about yourself. The entire third paragraph takes the general meaning of the teacher's actions and makes it personal, thereby providing more insight into the student.

Another student in Mr. Anderson's music department could have experienced the same things but appreciated them for different reasons – or not appreciated them at all. This personal discussion is what will distinguish this student's application from others in her school – and others in the applicant pool.

One shortcoming worth additional discussion is the brief mention of Mr. Anderson's illness at the end of the essay. It seems like his battling MS while remaining a committed teacher would have influenced the student more than his having taught her to respect the auditorium as a physical space. Sharing a story of how Mr. Anderson remained focused on his students during his illness and how that affected her would be more effective than discussing respecting space if it's true that this was more exceptional and therefore more meaningful to her. If not, then we wouldn't even mention the illness, since it becomes distracting to just drop it in and not discuss it.

Highly Competitive Essays

The following two pieces are exceptional application essays for the reasons indicated below. They also provide an example of how two essays on the "same topic" (the students' time with their fathers) are both completely different and also compelling because of the particular details that distinguish one student's unique experience from the other's (for a third example of this, see Chapter IV, section three where we've included a straightforward/factual essay that a student wrote about her father's illness inspiring her motivation).

Example 1:

Imagery – Puts us there in the airport with him, in the moment. Allows us to see what's happening to this student and to sympathize with him while it's happening. This immediacy gives a face – and a voice – to the story many of us have only heard about in less personal summaries.

Holding my cheeks with his hands firmly while gazing into my eyes; my father said, "Take care of your mother and sister and please promise me that you will study very hard, your education will be our way out of poverty." His moist eyes revealed tears fighting to be held back. He whispered to me, "Son, I love you, and I'm making this decision to provide you a better future. He kissed my forehead and quickly looked away as tears had begun flowing down his cheeks. I ran back to hug my mother and sister, and together we gazed at my father through the big windows of the airport.

Objective telling of his situation keeps the essay from slipping into sentimentality or trying to manipulate the reader's emotions (which can sometimes back-fire).

I grew up in one of the worst neighborhoods in Mexico City, Mexico. I vividly remember my surroundings at a young age and the struggle of living in deep poverty. **I have a crystal clear memory of when** *my mother would take us to have dinner with the neighbors because she couldn't afford to place food on our table that night. I can recall the fear that my sister and I had to share every time my mother left home for work.* **Shootings and crime were very prominent and widespread throughout the neighborhood.**

These details – again, shared in a neutral, objective way – personalize the essay and allow readers insight into the student's experience.

Life brightened when my father brought us to the United States after four endless years. Luckily, we no longer had to beg for food or sell my clothes to get a warm meal.

Again, these specific, personal details help us begin to know the student and the environment from which he's come.

Because of my upbringing, I feel that I was pre-destined to fail. This likelihood regarding my future made me shiver but it also filled me with passion to prove that I could overcome adversity, and that I could convert my struggles into a reason to succeed, rather than an excuse to fail.

Speaks to the student's character and initiative that he chose to work that much harder.

One late afternoon, I persistently attempted to wake my father up so that together we could complete my third-grade homework assignment. Using an old English-Spanish dictionary, my father and I used to lie down on the carpet to translate my entire homework assignment word by word. We sure missed Google-Translator. **But that night my father did not wake up due to his fever.** *"Son, try it on your own, I'll be there in a few."*

Speaks to the relative ease that we now have through software…and that many have through studying in their native language. In addition, the quick, well placed joke lets us know this student has kept his sense of humor despite the challenges he's faced, which tells us a lot about his personality and resilience.

This description backs up the picture of a third grader on his own that the last paragraph has set up for us. It also reveals character and personality, as the student is courageous enough to honestly describe the emotions he was experiencing.

I became shocked; panic rushed through my bloodstream and my body's temperature dropped. Never before had I completed a homework assignment on my own. Feeling frightened and isolated, I opened the cover page of the dictionary with a bit of anxiety.

That day marks a pivotal point towards my interest for learning, my love for understanding, and my passion for discovering. Although it may have taken me four hours to complete a twenty-minute assignment, I, for the first time, felt accomplished; I felt success and I felt instant pride which captivated me completely.

To see my mother and father release tears of joy for what they called "my bravery" was my first taste of success. They were proud, but not more proud than I was.

His gentle mocking of his third-grade accomplishment shows us that he doesn't take himself too seriously, while also demonstrating that he understands the very real impact of this milestone moment. Discusses intellectual curiosity, drive and resilience while still remaining humble.

This student's emotional honesty and specific details make us feel like he's inviting us to know more about his intimate thoughts and motivations. He admits and takes responsibility for the potentially negative emotions as much as he shares the positives of his situation, which rings true. Many essays that just tell us what people think we want to hear focus fully on the positive aspects, which has the effect of being forced and false. This student seems more focused on trying to share his experience than on spinning it. He also describes it in detail so we're there with him, which allows us to interpret the events rather than having him interpret them for us. At the same time, he responds to selection criteria. While discussing a momentous experience and being humorous and personal, his essay also illustrates academic achievement (and motivation), overcoming adversity and strong character.

Example 2:

Establishes the continuity of what we're about to hear. This is a normal, recurring activity for this student.

Sunday Best

Subverts expectations in calling work clothes "Sunday best." This engages the reader from the outset.

It is a typical evening in July. I have on my Sunday best, a shirt with a fraying collar and a pair of my dad's faded Levi's. My shoes are still caked in mud from last weekend's venture, a two-day endeavor laying stone pavers in the backyard.

Out of the Subaru, I pull a worn, mustard-yellow dolly with wheels crudely secured by mismatched nuts and bolts while my dad loads the

Great detail that allows us to see the action.

Implies this is an accomplishment of his dad's that this student is proud of, and also connects to his own long-held goal, as we see later.

Parallelism links this student to his dad, indicating the impact his father has had on his life and goals. The specific detail again allows us to picture the scene but also calls to mind the endearing boy who wrote it and clearly loved his dad so much – not to mention the father who hung it proudly.

Again draws from his dad's example, while also illustrating his humility.

This phrasing establishes the projects as a meaningful shared experience between father and son. "Customary" activities are traditions, "thinking back" suggests nostalgia, and calling up the Eagles engages our senses further so we, too, can experience the atmosphere of nostalgia for these project days.

This student's choice to share this story about how he learned from his dad is much more effective than just telling us "I learned a lot from him" or "He taught me so much." Specificity and imagery are compelling skills to employ.

Vivid image that indicates he, too, is older. Elegant way to indicate the passing of time.

We FEEL this because we already know how meaningful this day has been to the student. We are there with him.

Even more, his dad believes in his chosen career path and ability to succeed.

cabinet we assembled yesterday. *Office projects have become customary for my dad and me. I think back to the late nights spent painting, installing equipment, making renovations always listening to the usual: my dad's favorite, The Eagles.*

As we enter my dad's office, an LED sign greets us: Welcome to Kimura Orthodontics, the realization of a goal he had since seventh grade. Similarly, in his private office hangs a sign of my own, a picture I drew in kindergarten that reads: "When I grow up, I want to be a detes (dentist). I want to roc (work) with Dad. I want to tech cis (teach kids) how to besh ther teth (brush their teeth)." To me, becoming an orthodontist is one of my goals, a means of bringing a smile to people's faces both literally and figuratively.

This Sunday we are putting up a 60-pound cabinet. We start taking measurements, drawing pencil lines on the clean walls. *As he usually does, my dad reminds me to measure twice and drill once.* I appreciate his advice. During our first father-son project, my dad cautioned me to not touch the drill. However, being a curious five-year-old, I disregarded his guidance and quickly found out that you should not handle a drill bit that has just been used.

Today, we still have the Craftsman drill, *which now dons a suit of duct-tape armor.* My dad pulls it out and begins slowing punching into the drywall. Realizing that our toggle bolts are too large for the holes, my dad switches to a larger countersinking bit. When it comes time to mount the cabinet, we run into difficulty holding it up on the wall. *Trying to employ my dad's effortless problem solving,* I notice some storage boxes on the floor and stack them on a desk to support the cabinet. My dad lets me screw the cabinet into the wall using an electric screwdriver that has long since run out of batteries.

As we leave the office, late as always, the hallway is empty. All the suites are dark inside with only the hall sconces giving off light. *My dad slaps me on the back and with a firm grip on my shoulder and tells me good job.* My small contribution of stacking the storage boxes did not go unnoticed. As the elevator doors open, my dad in his understated, sincere tone tells me, *"One day, you will be the orthodontist patients will come to see at Kimura Orthodontics."* Inside, I smile, wondering when our next office project will be.

This student essay tells us a moving story about his relationship with his father, while also giving us honest (not superficial or heavy-handed) insight into his intellectual motivation and goals, as well as conveying atmosphere, imagery and character. His is an example of how to write effectively about another person because he related his relationship with and respect for his father to his own life, goals and aspirations. If he hadn't provided some information as to why he chose to write about his dad, the essay could easily have become a biography of his father without any insight into why this student found him compelling or admirable.

Instead, reviewers could tell the difference between this student's essay about his dad and hundreds of other students' essays about their dads (including the previous examples) because he spent focused time discussing why his father was important to him in his distinct, specifically descriptive essay. Similarly, the fact that he shared such details as the picture he drew that hangs in his father's office helps us to visualize the picture and therefore him, both of which lead him to stand out in our memories.

5. AVOID THESE COMMON ESSAY MISTAKES THAT MAKE REVIEWERS WANT TO POKE THEIR EYES OUT

You want to write a stellar essay—one that not only conveys your personality with eloquence, but that also fully addresses the prompt. As reviewers, we want to be moved, surprised, shaken out of our application-reading comas. So how do you achieve this? One of the easiest ways to write a compelling essay is, surprisingly, by simply avoiding the following mistakes that we and our colleagues gripe about year after year. We've described the top five essay mistakes that we see here.

Mistake #1: Student Reiterates Transcript/Résumé

In all our years of experience in admissions, scholarships and grantmaking, one of the saddest moments is reading a short-answer response or essay that turns into a list of accomplishments, grades and classes. Don't fill your valuable essay space with information that can easily be found in the activity section of your application or on the transcript we've asked you to provide. If you do mention something that is already in another part of the application, you should do so intentionally, providing fresh insights. Maybe you're the head of a number of school clubs. An exploration of how this teaches you leadership and time management would be much better than simply listing the clubs and all of your responsibilities.

Mistake #2: Students write more about the person important to them than themselves

Remember when we wrote those essays about our role models in sixth grade? They all sounded the same because they focused on biographical details of the role model. Selection committees don't care to learn still more minutiae about the life and times of Abraham Lincoln, Margaret Thatcher or even your Grampa Joe. These people aren't applying for college or scholarships. You are. Make sure that you and what you've learned from the other person are the focus of your personal essay.

Mistake #3: Writes more about issue than themselves

Similarly, issue-based essays provide a great opportunity for applicants to demonstrate their passion for a cause. Many times, however, these essays end up focusing entirely on the issue at the expense of cutting the applicant out of the story. Your essay may make a solid argument that the stagnating income of middle-class Americans is a serious threat to long-term economic growth, but you have to spend at least half of the essay discussing your role in addressing this issue and explaining why it influences your life in particular. Otherwise, reviewers will feel like they read a generic newspaper article rather than having gained any new insights into you as a person.

Mistake #4: Writes more about what happened than its significance

Don't build up the tension with a great story that never ties back to its effect on you as a person. Leaving the selection committee with a giant "SO WHAT?!" at the front of their minds will not help your chances of being admitted or of receiving a scholarship. Instead, think of the 40-60 rule; roughly 40 percent what happened, 60 percent how you have changed or grown from living this experience. The key is to recount your experiences just enough that your reader knows what happened and then to spend the bulk of your time reflecting and sharing the meaning you've derived from those experiences.

Mistake #5: Writes about challenges but remains broken

Challenges and obstacles can be some of the more compelling elements of a college or scholarship application—that is, if the applicant is able to demonstrate how they've overcome their circumstances and grown as a person. You may be wondering if it is a good idea to include tragic events or express heavy emotions when retelling difficult parts of your life. It is, if the large remainder of your essay focuses on how you've changed as a result of them. Often this growth is hinted at but not explored because the obstacle itself seems to be more dramatic. That might be true for Hollywood, but we're looking for your personal insights, and those can only come after the fact.

VIII. YOU HAVE EVERYTHING YOU NEED

Congratulations!

Your application package as a whole is solid.

You've peeked behind the curtain of each section of the college and scholarship application process, dispelling the mystery and getting clear on who you are and what you want to communicate.

You've articulated what you love and why, embraced your quirks and shared them with enough detail that reviewers can see and appreciate them – and therefore scc and appreciate you.

It takes a lot of self-awareness, as well as a lot of time and effort, to tell your story as effectively as you have.

And it takes a lot of courage to embrace all the various parts of your personality – much less write about them and share them with strangers. In this, you have already succeeded.

As you hit save for the last time, or finally click the submit button on each application, we wish for you an understanding of the depth of your accomplishment, as well as a fuller appreciation of who you are and what you want out of life.

As you wait to hear back from institutions, revel in triumph. You've earned it.

IX. ACKNOWLEDGMENTS

We are profoundly thankful for our scholar assistants who have been critically helpful at various stages of the drafting and editing of this book. Matt Iritani for all of his research and advice, Garrett Mayberry for his earnest suggestions and insights, Maddie Doering for her perspective and productive humor, Ashlyn Stewart for her eagle eye and immense speed – and all four of them for their enduring encouragement, patience and contributions. We could not have done this without you.

We would also like to thank Samantha Cure, Amelia Davis and Maithreyi Gopalakrishnan for sharing their viewpoints on their own college and scholarship application processes, as well as David Chan for providing a true high school senior's perspective on the numerous current resources on college and scholarship selection processes. Immense gratitude to Analise Iwanski for her design work in support of our marketing efforts.

Tracy Thompson, Dan Baum, Rena Maez and Adam Silver have our deepest gratitude for allowing us to benefit from their expertise through their close reading and insightful comments that were critical to the clarity and usefulness of the book. Eric Wilder for the clever and beautiful design of our cover and layout, which visually support the content so well.

In addition, we would like to thank the Boettcher Foundation Board of Trustees, our students who provided the inspiration and examples for this book, our work colleagues (in particular, Tim Schultz, Tiffany Anderson, Stephanie Panion, Kristi Arellano, Marisa Pooley and Audra Palakodety, who each had particular roles in bringing this project to fruition).

And, of course, any list of acknowledgments would be incomplete without thanking all of our colleagues in admission and scholarship selection processes over the years, as well as our spouses and families, including our parents, as all have supported us and specifically helped with this book in various ways.

X. ABOUT THE AUTHORS AND THE FOUNDATION

Katy Craig has worked professionally with higher education selection processes for 17 years. This includes those for college admission, honors and leadership programs, and various national and regional scholarships. She is also a national and international speaker on leadership and on personal and professional development.

Katie Kramer is president and CEO of the Boettcher Foundation, where she leads the philanthropic organization in both scholarship and grantmaking work. Katie served as the foundation's first scholarship director and was instrumental in establishing the processes and systems the foundation continues to use. As a board member of the National Scholarship Provider's Association, Katie frequently shares best-practices and other guidance with scholarship providers throughout the country.

Founded in 1937, the Boettcher Foundation invests in the promise of Colorado and the potential of Coloradans. The Boettcher Scholarship supports Colorado's top students by providing them with Colorado scholarships to attain an excellent in-state education, a vast network of alumni and community leaders and access to additional opportunities that enrich their time in college. Since 1952, the Boettcher Foundation has awarded nearly $100 million in undergraduate scholarships to many of Colorado's best and brightest students. That translates to more than 2,400 current and alumni Boettcher Scholars. Annually, more than 1,500 students apply for the 42 available Boettcher Scholarships.

Made in the USA
Las Vegas, NV
01 November 2022

58578700R00063